ESCAPE FROM THE PLASTIC PRISON

A Practical Guide to Getting Yourself Out of Debt!

> It's a great pleasure to get to know you, Matt. I'm marveling at some of the parallels that can be drawn regarding our lives. One example — look at our books' back cover! LOL. Looking forward to seeing you and Julia ASAP!
>
> Warmest regards, Brother,
>
> Benn

By Benn Perry

Copyright © 2011 by Benn Perry

All rights reserved.

No part of this publication may be reproduced, stored in a retrieval system or transmitted in any form or by any means; electronic, mechanical, photocopying, recording, scanning or otherwise, without the express written consent of its author.

ISBN 978-1460970126

To order this book, contact your local bookstore or online at:

www.CreateSpace.com/3574280

Proudly made in the USA – Charleston, South Carolina

Cover Design – Andrea Perrine Brower
    APB Illustration & Graphic Communication

DEDICATION

To Mom and Dad for setting wonderful life examples; for their incomparable business savvy, innate sense of knowing that we are here to help others and for walking the walk by and through their commitment and unwavering dedication to a national service that was the epitome of what credit counseling once was.

TABLE OF ASSISTANCE

Opening Statement..1

Before I begin – these two stories need to be told..............12

Chapter 1   It's apparently in my blood........................23

Chapter 2   Nobody WANTS to be in debt....................42

Chapter 3   My kingdom for a budget........................49

Chapter 4   Talking can be good, but..........................64

Chapter 5   More about bankruptcy............................110

Chapter 6   The infomercialization of America..............127

Chapter 7   There ought to be a law............................139

Chapter 8   Credit repair clinics.................................165

Chapter 9   Third party reporting agencies..................173

Chapter 10   The courtroom isn't just for lawyers............186

Chapter 11   Credit card fraud....................................200

Chapter 12   The "Bailout" wasn't enough? 206

Chapter 13   Don't fall for the offers to reestablish...........218

Chapter 14   What's next? 225

Chapter 15   In summary...238

OPENING STATEMENT

You do not need a credit counseling agency to get you out of debt!

How's that for an opening statement?

I spent nearly three decades helping American consumers get out of debt through our family-founded organization - Credit Counselors Corporation. Almost weekly, someone would ask *"What is it that you do that debtors cannot do for themselves?"* And each time it was asked, I responded similarly by saying *"Nothing, really."*

But you could ask that question of any person in any profession, couldn't you? I mean, given the right physical and mental tools anyone could fix their own car, build their own computer, market their own company and so on.

However, since walking away from that ever-expanding arena in 2002, I've had plenty of time to reflect on that question, and although I'd written a great deal of this book years earlier, I decided to update it, add anecdotes and provide everyone that reads it with the information they need to get themselves out of debt.

I have no regrets about my tenure as the director of CCC, don't get me wrong. We helped tens, perhaps hundreds of thousands of people get their financial lives back on track, prevented countless bankruptcy filings and in general restored across-the-board sanity to folks who thought they'd either lose their homes, minds or will to live - due to the heavy burden that personal indebtedness put upon them.

For the first 20 years of industry-leading services, our services were provided to debtors absolutely FREE. There were no "suggested" donations asked of our clients, no monthly "contributions" sought; in other words not a single penny was ever required of our clients.

That was possible because our financial support came directly from our clients' creditors who realized that without our intervention they might never collect their money, and, it was their most profitable alternative for reducing their losses. It's ALWAYS a money issue, especially with banks and credit card companies. The bottom line is ALWAYS *their* bottom line!

But with the infusion of deep-pocket funding of what I eventually called "industry marauders," it became impossible to sustain our services solely by the contributions we received from the creditors; because at some point the stance was taken that there were so many entities becoming involved in the industry that it only made sense for them to reduce their rate of contribution.

Eventually, toward the end of the 1990's, legislation was enacted that allowed counseling agencies to charge "nominal" or "minimal" fees (AKA contributions) to their debtor clients. The use of the word contribution was handy and almost philanthropic sounding, but, candidly, that flew in the very face of the principles upon which our organization was built. How, we reasoned, can you expect to help someone get out of debt by saddling them with yet another monthly expense? No matter what we'd choose to call it, it was a service fee, and it just seemed wrong!

Then, fledgling companies managed to convince the powers-that-be (who to this day are still unknown to this author) that "accreditation" was necessary in order to ensure that a credit counseling agency was "doing the right thing!"

It didn't matter that our organization had been helping consumers get out of debt free of charge for two solid decades, that we had returned on average six to seven million dollars per year to the credit industry…if we were not going to take part in the "mandatory" accreditation process; we were not going to be allowed to survive.

It was shortly after having that proverbial gun held to our heads (in the form of having to pay upward of $15,000.00 annually for accreditation) that I decided I'd had enough of the industry, one that, when born, was a marvelous alternative to bankruptcy and a tremendous help in relieving the mental anguish associated with trying to carry an overwhelming debt load.

Call it stubbornness or a sheer unwillingness to conform to the status quo, but it was time for yours truly to move on, professionally speaking.

In the years since my departure from the credit counseling industry I've performed a great deal of new and existing business consulting, helping with startups and lecturing here and there. I've been keeping a watchful eye on the industry that I recently predicted "might last another ten years at the most" and, frankly, with all the bad press it has received - the beginning of its end might already be here.

So it is most timely for me to share with you, in the form of this book, *practically* (I say practically because I'm not pompous enough to believe that there isn't a scintilla of information I don't know or even overlooked) everything you need to know about getting yourself out of debt; from letter writing, to the proper way of conversing with collectors, to your rights under federal legislation - to living a life free of credit card and other debt.

On April 20, 2005 new bankruptcy laws were passed and are contained within a 228 pages tome titled the Bankruptcy Abuse Prevention & Consumer Protection Act (BAPCPA) that made it more difficult for the average Joe or Jane to file Chapter 7 or Chapter 13 Bankruptcy.

What happened was people were considering filing personal bankruptcy as a first resort rather than a last resort, and there were countless loopholes in the existing legislation that made it easy to do so. As a result more and more debtors were abusing the system; which clearly hurt those that were trying their level best to make restitution on their outstanding credit obligations. How? Interest rates were hiked with very little notice or I should say without most consumers taking notice. Bank fees, over limit fees and every other imaginable fee were increased and there wasn't anything a soul could do about it.

In 1998, for the first time in our nation's history, one million consumers filed personal bankruptcy. By 2004 filings spiked to 1.6 million. Something had to be done, or so thought Congress and the major players in the industry, and the BAPCPA was passed.

The new Act created a momentary boon for counseling agencies because a major part of the legislation states that an individual cannot file bankruptcy without first consulting a "certified" credit counseling agency.

And, ironically, the government's certification process is not far removed from the "accreditation" process which coincidentally, or not, just so happens to have grandfathered in all of the agencies that received accreditation from one of those new organizations that "appear" to be government funded - like the one that I bucked nearly a decade ago now.

The difference is that the BAPCPA is administered through the office of the Trustee at the United States Department of Justice; much more organized and scary sounding from a small business person's perspective, I must admit.

The best thing to be said about this book, in my opinion, is that with the exception of the price you paid for it, you won't have to surrender any fees ever again to counseling agencies, and, very likely, you won't have to file bankruptcy.

When news of this book spreads throughout the counseling industry it will create quite a stir. There are literally thousands of credit counseling agencies that will have their coffers seriously depleted when their clients jump ship and do what they know they're capable of doing…get themselves out of debt!

I refuse, however, to live in fear of personal reprisal, because my conscience tells me that this information is more important today than ever before; and I feel it is my obligation, or calling if you will, to provide it to the masses.

By the mere actions of the banks that have benefited from billions of dollars of taxpayers' money in the form of the infamous "BAILOUT" (much more on that later) you won't catch me crying if they never hold a single benefit on their behalf.

The right feet never seem to be held to the fire when it comes to the tactics and hidden charges credit card companies pull off at the expense of we law-abiding and honest taxpaying citizens, and for them to be finally held accountable, if in only a small way, by the administration, speaks volumes of the effort to keep them in check by President Obama, and for that I am most grateful.

I also have confidence that the present administration will consider my book to be in concert with its effort to stimulate economic growth; by saving consumers countless millions in unnecessary monthly fees paid to agencies that, when all is said and done, do very little to effect positive change on behalf of their debtor clients.

Of course, no one wants to be in debt, but it truly can happen to anyone. A miles long list can be compiled of "famous" people that have had to bite the financial bullet at some point in their lives prior to becoming known for their success.

I don't know if it will make you feel any better to know some of their names, but, as a matter of public record, on the next page you'll find my Top 60 list of celebrities whose stars didn't shine so brightly at one point in their careers and ended up filing bankruptcy.

1. Abraham Lincoln
2. Al Jolson
3. Andy Gibb
4. Anita Bryant
5. Anna Nicole Smith
6. Bernard Goetz
7. Billy Sims
8. Bjorn Borg
9. Bob Guccione
10. Burt Reynolds
11. Buster Keaton
12. Cathy Lee Gifford
13. Charles Goodyear
14. Cyndi Lauper
15. Daniel DeFoe
16. David Crosby
17. Debbie Reynolds
18. Dino DeLaurentis
19. Don Johnson
20. Donald Trump
21. Donald Trump (Twice)
22. Eddie Fisher
23. Francis Ford Coppola
24. Frank Baum
25. Gary Burghoff
26. George Fiderich Handl
27. Heidi Fleiss
28. Henry Durant
29. Jerry Lewis
30. Johannes Gutenberg
31. John Barrymore
32. John Connelly
33. John James Audubon
34. John Wayne Bobbitt
35. Johnny Unitas
36. Kim Basinger
37. Larry King
38. Lenny Bruce
39. Leon Spinks
40. Margot Kidder
41. Marvin Gaye
42. Mickey Rooney
43. Miguel DeCervantes
44. Milton Hershey
45. Nelson Bunker Hunt
46. Nikola Tesla
47. Oscar Wilde
48. Oskar Schindler
49. P. T. Barnum
50. Peter Bogdonovich
51. Phoebe Snow
52. Redd Foxx
53. Rembrandt VanRijn
54. Samuel L. Clements
55. Thomas Alva Edison
56. Walter Elias Disney
57. Wayne Newton
58. William C. Durant
59. Willie Nelson
60. Zsa Zsa Gabor

I don't know about you, but it made *me* feel better to see those names...because they ultimately were not known for their temporary personal financial lapses, and because, like you, should bankruptcy be your only option *(and you'll know if it is by the time you finish this book)* you too will come out of it alright.

Without "official" psychologist's credentials, but armed with decades of first-hand experience in dealing with individuals, couples and entire families on a face-to-face basis, I can speak to you as therapeutically as can your neighborhood tavern's bartender when it comes to the issue of personal indebtedness, or what I call the lack of sound "fiscal fitness."

I've literally watched grown men and women breakdown in tears at the very mention of their outstanding credit and medical obligations.

I've seen monumental denial displayed by credit card abusers that are unwilling to recognize that they and they alone are the reason they are in deep debt.

I've witnessed verbal abuse heaped on debtors by bill collectors from national collection agencies that would make sailors blush.

I've conducted counseling sessions centered on the question of wants versus needs and strove to teach people how to understand and differentiate between the two.

I cannot begin to tell you how many hours I've spent trying to diffuse arguments between spouses over unknown items that were purchased on credit, or worse, not knowing that the other even had a specific credit card at all.

But most importantly, I've been around the business long enough to know that the vast majority of debtors are honest citizens that happen to fall upon hard times, and that the reasons for their debt, while varied, come about not by choice and often out of sheer survival instinct.

For every reason, and for every season that has passed that saw me ministering to my credit counseling minions, one thread seems to have been inextricably woven through the fabric that makes up the debtor; *embarrassment*.

It is an understandable feeling, and one with which I can personally empathize. As I mentioned, debt can happen to anyone and it happened to yours truly as well. But in following that sage's advice who once said to follow ones own advice, I did just that. By taking the bull by the horns, I am happy to report that even in these difficult economic times, I am living debt free; as will you - once you've followed this step-by-step process.

So, enough about how it happened, enough beating yourself up over it; it's time to take *charge* (*pun intended*) of your financial situation, once and forever.

You did not get into debt overnight and there is no "quick fix" out there regardless of the number of infomercials that insist otherwise; however this book is a sensible and proven approach that takes practically every condition into account and allows you to put your personal recovery plan into action immediately.

The first step to getting yourself out of debt is cutting up ALL of your credit cards; just like the guy on the cover!

Sounds simple, but if you're determined, for whatever reason, to still be a "user," you might just as well put this book down right now - because as long as you are still charging you will NEVER get out of debt. That is an undeniable statement and one that is true 100% of the time.

Your creditors would never tell you that because they want you to be indebted to them for the rest of your natural days.

Perform plastic surgery of your own right now. Painful as the first cut might be, by the time you finish the last one on the final card the air of emancipation will instantly take over your spirit.

Then and only then will you be ready to begin planning the escape from your plastic prison!

BEFORE I BEGIN – THESE TWO STORIES NEED TO BE TOLD

It was October 19, 1987, a day that will forever be remembered as "Black Monday." The day the stock market crashed.

Like most adults, this is one of those dates where you have little or no difficulty recalling where you were and what you were doing when it occurred; from both a personal and career standpoint.

For me, it was memorable for a number of reasons.

Whenever anyone asks me where I was on "Black Monday" I instantly tell them "I was in Chicago taping an appearance on "The Oprah Winfrey Show." It's true, and the story you are about to read is also true.

CCC was in its 12th year of existence (Oprah was in her second year of broadcasting then) when I received an invitation to appear on *The Queen of Daytime Talk's* television show. Earlier in the year we were contacted and asked if we would furnish a couple of clients to come on the show to talk about their personal financial plights, in order to explain to Americans how grave peoples' situations could get, and, I thought, to let them know that there was a light at the end of the tunnel in the form of our counseling service.

Being somewhat naïve, and presuming that nothing but good could come from this, I acquiesced and provided a husband and wife that were happy to go on national TV to tell their story.

But their story was not one of blatant misuse of credit cards; far from it. Their story was one that rarely gets headlines, rarely receives national attention and usually doesn't crop up in the same conversation as credit card debt.

Bill and Cindy Roberts were in debt because Bill was diagnosed with cancer and due to a combination of Insurance company snafus and the feeling that nobody gets cancer in their early thirties, they got behind the eight ball by using credit to pay "living" expenses (including rent, food, electricity, etc.) and medical bills. It got to the point where they could no longer keep robbing from Peter to pay Paul and it clearly made no sense at all for them to try to pay medical bills with high interest-bearing credit cards.

I implore you to never use credit to pay medical bills. I'll elaborate on that in a later chapter, but you simply should NEVER do it!

Getting back to Bill and Cindy's story; they did a wonderful job on the show. They told their tale with aplomb and class and anyone who watched it had to have come away with the feeling that their own situation wasn't *that bad* and that there was hope out there, that credit counseling was a positive alternative to bankruptcy and quite possibly the answer to their most pressing problems.

Several months passed when I received a phone call from one of Oprah's staffers that essentially went like this: "I'm calling for Christine Tardio, Oprah's producer, and the show we did earlier in the year with Bill and Cindy Roberts went so well that we would like you to send a few more of your clients to us for a similar show. But this time we'd like people that are in credit card debt."

My response: "I will be happy to provide you with a few more clients under one condition; that you also invite me to appear on the show so that I can throw a lifeline to the millions that are watching that might be in debt. The last show might have been great for Oprah's ratings, but as far as I know, not one person benefitted from it outside of your studio audience because I never heard a word about it from a single consumer."

To which the woman replied "That sounds like blackmail to me." I said "Call it what you will, but unless the objective is to HELP people I see no reason to return, with or without a few of our clients." "I'll get back to you" she said.

An hour later I received a call back advising me I was on the guest list.

Fast forward to Sunday, October 18, 1987, the day I flew up to Chicago and the day before the show's scheduled taping.

It was around 6:00PM – I was preparing to meet my two clients, Teresa Caldwell and another woman that shall remain nameless (at her request). Incidentally, it was never our practice to share any names of CCC clients or information about them to anyone other than their creditors, naturally, but when it came to national television appearances, Bill and Cindy before her, and Teresa, had no problems revealing their actual personae. I don't know, maybe it was that desire to have their Andy Warhol *15 minutes of fame*, but they were okay with it.

I received a call in my hotel room at the Chicago Hilton & Towers, which was the same room that President Lyndon B. Johnson chose to stay in when he was in town visiting in the winter of 1964. After the bellhop conveyed that information to me, I remember sarcastically saying, "Well, then if it was okay for President Johnson, I guess it'll be okay for me."

Anyway, the call comes in and after I answered it the voice on the other end of the line, in a rather mysterious tone, said "Is this Benn Perry?" "Yes, it is. Who is this?" I replied. Without providing identifying information he went on: "I'm with a group from Cicero." I later learned that Cicero was meant to instill fear in me for the common knowledge that it was a Chicago area Mafia hotbed. It did not instill fear in me, at first, because I had no idea about the town's nefarious roots.

"It has come to our attention that you are going to be a guest on *The Oprah Winfrey Show* tomorrow, is that correct?"

"That's right" I said. He continued "If you value your life and the life of your wife and young son in Davie, Florida, DON'T DO IT!"

Then he hung up the phone! He didn't slam down the receiver, he simply terminated the call, rather gracefully and quite matter of fact; as if he'd made calls like that on many other occasions.

What would you do next?

After my internal freaking out process subsided, after all the thoughts of my imminent death and notions of impending doom for my entire family abated *somewhat*, I took logical stock of the situation and did what I surmise most unassuming and frightened humans would do, I called hotel security.

Hotel security was fantastic. They knew I was not only one of *their* guests but they also knew I was a scheduled guest on the *Oprah Show* the next morning. Together we tried to determine who might make such a threatening telephone call to me. Had I any enemies? Had I provoked anyone recently?

I never provoked anyone, that's just not my style. Had I threatened to say or do anything on *Oprah* that might cause others aggravation, embarrassment or consternation? I had to answer a resounding NO to all of those questions.

I was just a little not-so-old business professional that was going to go on the air to help people; what was so wrong with that?

Apparently that wasn't good enough for the Chief of Hotel Security or the management of the Chicago Hilton & Towers, and I was glad it wasn't. He contacted the police and in short order there we were, in my hotel room; me, the Chief of Hotel Security and a very high ranking officer of the Cook County Police Department in a powwow.

My excitement about my national TV appearance had gone from the most thrilling and positive career moment to one of dread and heightened fear. By this time I was clued in to the Cicero reference, as you might imagine.

We couldn't figure out why anyone would want to threaten my life and my family's lives - and nobody was leaving that room until we did.

A battery of questions was fired at me, to the point where I felt as though I was the one that had better come up with answers quickly; as if I were a suspect.

And then my answer to the following question opened the eyes of all in attendance: "Why are you appearing as a guest on the show tomorrow?" the officer queried. I explained that I was going there to share the lifeline that is CCC to anyone and everyone within eye and earshot of *The Oprah Winfrey Show*; to tell her viewers how we can help them get out of debt, and, here's the kicker...that our services were FREE OF CHARGE to consumers.

Simultaneously a light went on in both Chiefs' heads and the Security Chief asked me if there was any reason why my giving that information would bother anyone, "say...your competition?"

My answer was then a resounding YES, because there were, at the time, many credit counseling agencies that charged fees for their services; the same services that I was about to go ON-AIR and offer to the nation FREE OF CHARGE!

Several events ensued that, believe it or not, were more harrowing than what you just read, and might appear to have come directly from a spy novel, but in the interest of staying on point it was concluded that this was merely a white collar attempt to discourage me from going on TV, and that, presumably, my appearance would mean the potential loss of millions of dollars in revenue to our rival and supposedly non-profit "competing" agencies.

I put the word "competing" in quotations because we never felt that helping our fellow man would be a competitive thing, and as long as owners of other credit counseling agencies had the same helpful mission statement in play as ours – there was enough room for anyone that wanted to be in the industry. Boy, were we ever rubes on that one!

I was nearly convinced that no harm would come to me by going on the show until I subsequently learned that Oprah's producer was also threatened by the anonymous voice on the phone – that if Benn Perry was "allowed to be on your show," they could "rest assured you'll get your broadcasting license pulled by the F.C.C." This, as a result of the complaint they planned to file with that governmental agency if I did make my appearance.

To her credit, Oprah personally expressed that there was no way any guest would be invited on her show without proper vetting beforehand and if they had "the goods" on Mr. Perry as they persisted, either produce it now or "he goes on!" They never came up with anything, obviously. Oprah realized it was just a corporate threat, and, as the saying goes, the show went on.

I had become lulled into a comfort zone at a point during the taping when a man from the audience, during the Q&A portion of the show, stood up beside Oprah and reached into the breast pocket of his suit coat. Holy crap, I thought to myself, this is IT. This is the guy. He's gonna pull out a gun and shoot me on national television. The scene from the movie *Network* flashed before my eyes; where the network executive planned on blowing his brains out on LIVE TV to garner the greatest ratings share of all time!

With sweat streaming over my face I frantically scoped my surroundings, trying to figure out where I might run for cover once the shots started flying. I knew that the fabric gray chair upon which I sat wouldn't absorb gunfire. Could I make it to the wings of the stage before getting winged by a well-aimed or wayward bullet? All these thoughts rushed through my brain and then the would-be assailant *pulled it out*.

It was *a piece of paper* with a planned question about, of all things, insurance. Never had anything so irrelevant to the topic at hand been such a welcome relief to me. Oprah asked the man what *that* had to do with personal indebtedness, I think, but I was thrilled to see a piece of paper and not a .357 Magnum yanked from his clothing.

Story Number Two:

The Oprah story takes me back to the start of why I feel the industry, which we at CCC basically co-founded, eventually became insidious and far from well-intentioned. Even though I'd experienced that hair-raising episode I remained naïve about the industry that I thought was inherently good - for two decades too long, I'm sorry to say.

Several years prior, my father was contacted by one now long since deceased man by the name of Harry Brown. Harry Brown was the director of the Miami office of Consumer Credit

Counseling Services, a *national* debt repayment service along the lines of what we were endeavoring to become at CCC.

You can add two and two together with respect to my Oprah experience and see if you come up with any conclusions for yourself here. But, I digress:

Mr. Brown did whatever persuading he could to convince my Dad not to get into this line of work. Seems he felt as though CCC would be "competition" and that wasn't something Harry wanted to deal with at the time.

Dad told Harry to go jump off a cliff, or harsher words to that effect. Harry didn't take him up on it; instead he hired an attorney by the name of William (Bill) Kruglak to do his dirty work. Do you find it coincidental that a bill collector's nickname might actually have been Bill?

Continuing: Kruglak, on his attorney's letterhead no less, and I'm paraphrasing now (although I retain the original letter as proof) insisted that if CCC did not cease and desist from the credit counseling business - bad things would happen to them   In follow-up phone calls which were taped for posterity, Kruglak actually threatened to have Dad's legs broken. My, my, what benevolence and love for our fellow man CCCS was displaying through its henchmen.

What do these stories have to do with you and your personal financial plight or how to get yourself out of debt? They were added so that you would have some frame of reference when I tell you now that of all the nasty, unsavory, under-worldly, devious and un-cool things I had to confront as an agent of hope as the National Director of a credit counseling agency *by others in that industry* – none can compare to the tactics I've seen and heard perpetrated against the public by bill collectors over the years.

For every horror story I can tell you, you probably can add one of your own. For every graphic detail of nerve and guile that could fill a book itself, you've likely gone through a similar experience with a bill collector on the phone or, dreadfully, in-person.

On that happy note, please do continue.

CHAPTER 1
IT'S APPARENTLY IN MY BLOOD

Some kids follow in their fathers' or mothers' footsteps, I am one of those kids. Since I was old enough to walk, my parents were involved in the collection end of this *game* called the credit industry. They owned and operated a collection agency for nearly twenty years, and prior to that, Dad worked as one of those guys that were referred to as a "street collector." That's correct; he literally journeyed into neighborhoods and knocked on debtors' doors. And here's the unbelievable part; he actually expected to get paid on the spot. Sometimes, believe it or not, he did!

As you might imagine, street collectors are a dead breed. I don't think it's because they were killed off, but Dad shared some hair raising stories that might make you suspect that was the reason for their inevitable extinction!

Prior to the 1970's, bill collectors got away with murder, not in the literal sense, but darn close to it. Their tenacity, badgering, ridiculing nature and vile tactics had virtually gone unchecked. In fact, so heinous were their approaches that public outcry led to federal legislation to assure consumers certain rights - and the legislation ensured they were protected under them.

That legislation is still called the "Fair Debt Collection Practices Act." (FDCPA), and it became law on March 20, 1978.

Under the Act, for a solid decade, collection agencies as well as credit grantors were forced to pay strict adherence to its tenets. Consumers "seemed" to be becoming more educated and less afraid of that once feared dinner time interruption in the form of a collection phone call. They knew they had rights. They were aware of what was considered harassing tactics and did not tolerate them.

But something uncanny happened, something that I cannot quite put a finger on; the nastiness came back, and it came back with a vengeance. Certainly the series of world events that have taken place, particularly the devastating tragedy of *September 11, 2001*, have forced the citizenry to focus more on foreign and domestic affairs relating to *personal security matters* and less on *personal financial matters*. Or, at least those other more serious events took precedence in the American psyche - and somehow, some way, the bullying beast known only as "the collector" has wormed his way back into our society.

Foul, they'll cry from the anonymity that their telephones provide, but today's bill collector is more vicious than ever before. It is unfair; however, to say just "he" has wormed his way back, because without a doubt, the most biting tones and creepiest tactics are those employed by none other than the female collector.

One can theorize as to why women make better collectors, or worse collectors, depending on your personal perspective.

If you are a debtor you probably have several reasons in mind. Oh, and if you are looking for political correctness among these pages you won't find it; because I've decided not to pull any punches. I would not be true to myself if I sugar-coated any parts of this project to protect the feelings of anyone other than the debtors in whose benefit this book was written.

In several forums I have debated the occasional bill collector that was brave enough to confront questions about their lack of compassion, or, more aptly put, their disturbing telephone demeanor. I even baited one to be a guest on a Cable Ace award-winning television show I produced and hosted called "Fiscal Fitness." Each time the debate would touch on their unwillingness to listen to reason (as they merely considered the dollars that were outstanding and not giving an ounce of forethought to the fact that they were speaking to actual human beings) it invariably ended with a comment akin to "Hey, it's just my job, man. Somebody's got to do it!"

Going entirely on personal experience, I've deemed that women make for more aggravating bill collectors. Having said that, think for a moment of the power a collector wields with phone in hand. She or he has the right to call total strangers in an attempt to get money from them. That is a very powerful weapon in the debt game.

I have always maintained that well over 90% of the bill collectors that comprise the debt collection industry are deeply in debt themselves.

It makes sense. Imagine what a relief, what an outlet it would be if you were in debt and could turn the anger you have for those trying to get money out of you - back on others. That is incredible empowerment to say the least.

So we have all these deeply indebted loose cannons firing off at unassuming debtors and it is, to abuse a sports metaphor...game on!

Anyone that has been in debt has heard one or more of the following collection agent commentaries:

"Well, we didn't lend money to a stone, so pay your bill!"
"Are you refusing to pay?"
"Then take out a loan!"
"Get a THIRD job then!"
"If you don't pay this bill we're going to take you to court!"
"Yeah, like I've never heard *that one* before!"

If you didn't have a personal stake in all of it, if you could listen to their prate from a disinterested third-party position, you'd probably bust out laughing.

One might be led to believe that there is some sort of school out there that collectors have to attend before they can officially be unleashed on the public; a sort of pit bull training compound or something.

Does the following scenario hit home?

Your neighbor receives a call they are told is **URGENT!** It is their "duty" as a neighbor, according to the caller, to deliver a message to you. The neighbor stops over and either verbally delivers the message, if you are unlucky enough to be at home when he comes calling, or leaves you this written message: "Some guy who says his name is Bill Doonow from Mastercard or Visa is trying to get hold of you and asked if you'd please call him at 1-800-PAY UP NOW.

Alright, so maybe they wouldn't be *that* bold, but what do they think your neighbor will surmise the call is all about? That's the whole idea as far as the wily veteran collector is concerned...getting you to the phone; even if it means embarrassing you in front of your neighbor - as if, as discussed earlier, you weren't embarrassed enough already.

Seriously, if my neighbor ran over with a similar kind of message, *I'd know he knew* I was behind with my creditors, and heaven knows the biggest secret guys ever keep from other guys is the fact that they are in financial trouble. "Great, now my buddy knows; it isn't bad enough that the whole family is suffering from our situation, now Joe knows too!"

I can sympathize *and* empathize with you, my friend. I have had to deal with those kinds of calls and *much worse*. And it doesn't matter that my background allows me to quote the law, chapter and verse, because the hardcore collectors do not fear reprisal.

I can state generally and without equivocation that bill collectors are a nasty breed of cat - because I have witnessed hundreds of them plying their craft from a cubicle or desk mere feet from my own. In twenty-eight years of running one of the most helpful credit counseling agencies in the United States I have run up against some of the most despicable, albeit creative individuals to ever lift a telephone's receiver to their ears.

I have had clients tell me that they were being pushed over the edge by these scathing individuals and if the non-stop bullying they were constantly receiving didn't cease; they were afraid they would snap. And I've seen some snap, and read about even more that couldn't stand the constant pressure, and, as a result, committed the worst crime of all, suicide. That's right; all because of words uttered by a stranger with, in most cases, less than a high school education - but possessing a dramatic flair for intimidating conversation.

It doesn't take much skill and it surely takes less empathy to become a collector. All you need is a voice and unfaltering nerve, even if you're only acting the part. In fact if a person has any degree of creativity they will thrive as a collector because he or she will implement new slogans or trash talking lines that their fellow workers will grow to revere and eventually adopt as their own; developing a shrewd and sarcastic technique while influencing others in the process. What a way to make people proud of you; he said tongue planted firmly in cheek.

But, necessity being the mother of all invention, from October of 1977 through January of 1980 *hypocritically as it now sounds, I was a bill collector,* employed by one of the largest credit card issuers in the world at the time; and the place wasn't Visa or Mastercard, or Master Charge as they were called back then either. It was a fortress-like facility in the Southeast Region of the U. S. that rhymes with *I'm there again, excess.*

And boy, I sucked at it! I sucked at being a bill collector (although we were called more poetically "account control analysts" then) because I couldn't summon the sarcasm or venom required to humiliate or belittle someone I'd never met. And even though I knew there had to be "another side of the story" my job was not to hear it, period. For some reason I was unable to speak to someone in a condescending manner; at least not someone I didn't know to deserve it.

I just could not bring myself to kick someone when they were down, which is essentially what the collector has to do. In short, I didn't have the heart or stomach for it.

I remember one guy I'll call George Robin (because that was his name) going as far as locating a debtor in the emergency room of a hospital to ask him for money. I could hardly believe my ears. "George!" I said. "Did you just actually call the dude right after he got out of surgery?" To which he replied "Hey, I skip-traced that son of a bitch and finally found him; you don't think I'm gonna just drop it, do ya?"

Looking back on that episode and knowing all that I do about the lower life form known as the collector, no, I didn't expect George to just "drop it!" In fact, that experience made such an indelible impression on me that years later I included it as a pivotal scene in the screenplay I wrote and am presently working on turning into a major motion picture, called **"PAST DUE!"** Check your local movie times at a theater near you real soon!

With one major exception, which I'll get into shortly, as mentioned in the introduction, there is absolutely nothing a credit counseling service can do for you that you cannot do for yourself.

The problem is we humans are shortcut takers. If we can take a quicker route to anything, we'll jump at the chance. If it's a shortcut that is dangerous or risky, doesn't matter, we take it anyway! If someone offers us help, usually we'll take it.

Now if someone offers us help that provides a shortcut...we've hit the jackpot. This theory applies to personal debt.

Most consumers are so embarrassed by being in debt that they are initially reluctant to seek help. I'd always been at the head of the class when it came to trying to allay the fear of being talked down to. That's the greatest trepidation; that someone we don't even know will pass judgment on us.

We like guidance but hesitate to ask for it. We fear judgment but if that fear melts away we have already begun to win; we then tend to lower our guard and willingly take the hand offering us salvation.

As noted prior, when we started our counseling service in 1975 our services were provided absolutely FREE to the debtor. You heard that correctly. "Well, then how did you get paid?" was a fair question we were constantly asked.

Our financial support came in the form of contributions from our clients' creditors. It took two solid years to get the credit industry to fully perceive our mission statement because the surface complaint would be "Why pay you to get our own money back?"

When credit granting institutions finally understood our reply, which was "Because not only can you write off whatever you contribute to a non-profit counseling service on your taxes, you'll be fostering good will among your customers by working *with* them to help them through their temporary financial predicament," we were off and running.

They started to see the merit in working with us because in the back of their minds they were thinking that once the individual debtor was paid off…they'd help them reestablish; you know, get them back in the soup once again, meaning they'd be right where they wanted to be – back in their wallets! Thus was created the vicious cycle that could only serve the creditors' best interest.

When we founded CCC, it was a novel concept, a cottage industry if you will. There was one agency in Washington, D.C. that was sprouting up new offices seemingly every day, calling itself a national service, and, well…there was us! Whenever people heard the words national and service in the same sentence they presumed that the other agency was a federally subsidized one; it was not and is not to this day.

No matter what happens in our lives the one thing that sets the human race apart from all other species is our ability to communicate through words. Yet, when it comes to dealing with debt we are dumbstruck more often than not. You may be the chief orator at work, you may captain your debate team in college, you may even be a politician who speaks for a living and earns votes based on your ability to relate to your constituents…so why do we clam up so tightly when personal finances is the broached topic? We just do. There must be studies out there that prove that human tendency, but let's just agree to agree on that one for now.

Back to *The Oprah Winfrey Show* for a bit of what was actually discussed during my visit:

Along with the two CCC clients who agreed to tell their story, Howard Ruff, the editor of Ruff Times (his financial newsletter) and a widely respected stock market analyst, was Oprah's other featured guest. Howard was your basic all-around investment guru.

My purpose for being a part of the show was to discuss credit counseling and how our organization helped get people out of debt. Howard was there to tell people what to do if they happened to have a little money to invest.

Ironically, that was the day that saw the worst single day drop in the Stock Market in the history of Wall Street; at least until the banking collapse of 2008.

Most of our debtor clients could not have cared less about what happened in the Stock Market; unless its performance would somehow serve to pay their rent or put a little food on the family table. Therefore, it seemed logical that my appearance on that particular day would have much wider appeal, than would Howard's; and it did. And it did by virtue of the fact that nearly 45 minutes of the hour was spent discussing personal indebtedness, much to my delight.

It was all Mr. Ruff could do to keep from crawling out of his own skin, as with each commercial break the stock market was plummeting faster than you could yell SELL! My feeling was he just wanted to get out of there as quickly as possible to attend to his business in Utah.

When asked by Oprah what he would do if he had a thousand dollars to invest, Howard was at first understandably reluctant, but then proffered this statement: "Well, the market is experiencing a degree of volatility at the moment, so if I had a thousand dollars I would probably invest it in precious metals, maybe silver."

That was a good answer. He acquitted himself well, considering his sweat had probably reached his socks as he learned the market was already down over 180 points…and it wasn't even 10AM yet.

His answer was on the heels of my pat response to Oprah's question: "Benn, for people that feel they are over extended with credit cards, what would you suggest they do?" Of course I ultimately responded by saying: "If you *think* you might be in trouble, you *already are in trouble* and perhaps there is something we at Credit Counselors Corporation can do to help you out. All you have to do is call our toll-free number!"

I know it was a shameless plug but if you don't toot your own horn, who else will?

I also knew Oprah was peaking in popularity (a level she's managed to maintain for a quarter century and counting) and that my appearance on her show that was to be seen by over 30 MILLION everyday folks would do wonders to boost business and serve to make us a national credit counseling force with which to be reckoned.

I also figured that as a result of having the chance to throw a theoretical, if not literal, lifeline to her viewers by offering our FREE services to any and all in need - I would reap an even greater spiritual reward.

There's just something about knowing you're helping your fellow man that helps you sleep soundly at night.

So CCC was on the map. The producers of the show mentioned they regretted not providing our toll-free phone number on the screen. For a solid two weeks after the show aired their switchboard received thousands of calls inquiring as to how one would go about receiving our services, or at least get in touch with our office.

The varying organizations that helped get people out of debt experienced exponential growth. They grew so quickly in fact that by 2011, the number of companies with branch offices or single office operations providing credit counseling, debt negotiating or debt settlement services was conservatively in excess of 3800.

The industry grew to the point where it was beginning to cannibalize itself. What once was a novel concept had evolved into a poorly regulated, back biting, deceptive, frequently fraudulent, self-righteous, gigantic group of rank amateurs who professed to be experts in the field; a field that had become comprised of fledgling millionaires whose money had placed them, practically overnight, in positions of extreme influence.

In fact, the turn that the credit counseling industry had taken is really what motivated me to write this book. Truth be told, **there's very little, if anything, that credit counselors can do for you that you cannot effectively do for yourself**. That is the THIRD TIME you've read that statement or words similar to it, for good reason. I want to make sure you feel the conviction with which I utter it!

The problem is most people don't have the intestinal fortitude or remotely enough ammunition in the form of knowledge to competently deal with their dilemma.

All you need is the desire to get out of debt…this book will show you how to do the rest; in a dignified, professional manner.

One question Ms. Winfrey asked threw me for a loop. At first I thought her to be capricious in asking it, and my answer, since this was a LIVE taping, was strictly spontaneous. It wasn't until nearly a dozen years later that I actually "got it!"

"Benn," she asked. "Have you ever been in debt? "No, no I haven't," was my simple reply.

Her next question: "Well, then…how can you help people get out of debt if you've never been in debt?"

I was stunned! After catching my breath and putting my tongue on hold momentarily, I went on to explain *how* our company *literally* helped people get out of debt.

What I initially thought to myself in a thoroughly defensive mode was: "How can *you* host your own talk show if you've not spent decades studying psychology or philosophy or graduated with honors from a recognized college of journalism?" Admittedly I was offended.

After all, her producers had checked and rechecked our credentials prior to inviting me to be her guest. And for some time afterward I was puzzled by that question. You don't need to own a broken down car to be a mechanic any more than you need to have experienced being in debt to help people get out of debt, with the right tools, of course.

But in a very *real* sense, I was wrong.

I'd spent years and years sitting across from people who were truly suffering incredible mental pains, as they wondered how in the world they would ever climb out from under their mountain of credit cards and medical bills. I thought, through osmosis somehow, I knew their anguish. I did not.

Unless we wear the shoes, we can't know what it's like. Without first hand experience, we cannot possibly conceive of another's sorrow or happiness and *this* is where I push my personal door ajar in an effort to relate to you directly.

Had I known then what I know now I would have worded my response in a much different way. It might have gone something like this: "Oprah, I don't know how it feels personally to be in debt. I do *see* the pain etched deeply in the faces of my clients every day as they sit across the desk from me. I try to ease that pain with my knowledge on the subject of debt and by extending a helping hand whenever possible through our service."

That's what I *should have said*, but then hindsight is always "20-20"...and *that* is another TV show altogether.

I am now a member of the "been there, done that" crowd. Having grown somewhat tired and frankly burned by and burned out in the credit counseling field, I decided to strike out further on my own. Actually, I don't think strike out is a good way to put it, since in the vernacular that's precisely what I did.

Remember I said there are hundreds of reasons, maybe thousands, why people find themselves mired in the abyss of personal debt? Well, mine was just one of them. Again, you are privy to this because I want you to know that I DO know your pain, and since misery loves company, or at least because no one wants to feel like they are alone in this credit crunch...I'm sharing my story. It's NOT an excuse...just MY story.

I became involved in a couple of business ventures, both of which failed miserably from a financial standpoint, and, believe it or not I would still attempt them over again because the ideas were creative, heartfelt and well thought out. In both cases, however, it was bad timing. They say if you can learn from your mistakes it was not a total loss...and I learned plenty.

You don't need to know too many of the particulars, except that in an eighteen month period I found myself in debt to the tune of approximately a hundred grand and the prospect of answering bill collection calls.

Sometimes bankruptcy is unavoidable.

Such was my situation. Certain elements had to come together at specific times in order for financial success to be achieved...they didn't. I ended up in bankruptcy court, filing Chapter 7, which is the complete liquidation of all discretionary debts.

I am not in the least bit proud of having to file. I struggled mightily with the thought that there I was...the National Director of one of the most respected credit counseling agencies in America, and *I was filing bankruptcy.* It's very likely that was the time I looked up celebrities that filed bankruptcy and the reason I said earlier that I was comforted by seeing a lot of the names on that list.

But what kind of a hypocrite did that make me? Oprah was right. How could I help people get out of debt if I was never in debt?

But in the seventeen years to date since having to take that plunge into the deep end of the bankruptcy pool I have been empathetic as opposed to sympathetic in my approach with individuals and families who seek my help. I share with them my experiences and am able to relate to them much in the same manner as I am with you in this book; and while the actual act is considered taboo by many, filing personal bankruptcy for me was both cathartic and emancipating.

Bankruptcy is considered such a taboo topic because, by most definitions, the word is synonymous with the word failure. You ran up bills and didn't pay them and it doesn't matter what the circumstances were. Oddly, it doesn't make any difference to your creditors either because to them you are just a 16-digit account number; maybe less.

Mind you, the people who sit high upon their horses looking down on others for what they consider to be grave indiscretions invariably come crashing to Earth much harder if and when hard times befall them. I know; I've eyeballed *them* from across my desk too.

By not dwelling too much on the past, we are able to get a fresh start toward the future. There is a reason why the slogan "seeking *relief* through personal bankruptcy" was coined. It is the exorcising of a major mental demon and can lead to successes beyond imagination…depending upon the frame of mind you adopt after the exorcism is performed.

Later on I will devote an entire chapter to bankruptcy; the *why* and *why nots* as well as the *if, when, who should* and *how* of it all.

Chapter 2
NOBODY WANTS TO BE IN DEBT...

...but it CAN happen to anybody. And I mean ANYBODY. If you're sitting there thinking you are the only soul who's lost his way along the twisting road of personal credit, take solace in the fact that nearly 70 Million Americans are in some form of discretionary debt. Discretionary meaning those bills above and beyond your typical "fixed living expenses," such as monthly rent or mortgage, car payment, insurances, groceries, etc.

For most, it just sort of sneaked up on them. For others, it snuck up on them. After a year or two of running to our favorite retailers yelling CHARGE, before we knew it, there was more month left than money.

How does the old saying go? "I can't be out of money; I still have more checks left!" That's a very clever axiom, but it still doesn't pay the bills.

We play the *"Rob from Peter to Pay Paul"* game and notice that Peter is now perturbed and Paul still isn't getting paid. We put on a valiant statement-juggling act, until the unthinkable occurs. Oops, we dropped one of them; flat out missed a payment one month. Like juggling a tennis ball an olive and a plugged in chain saw, the creditor you drop usually ends up being a relative of the chain saw. Because, whereas nobody WANTS to be in debt, no creditor WANTS to be the only one you didn't think strongly enough about paying.

We find ourselves in previously uncharted waters, pressed into answering questions asked by total strangers about a matter as deeply personal as our finances. And it is undeniably one of the most uncomfortable feelings connected to the entire human experience.

While the odds are high that our next door neighbor is in the same sinking boat as we are when it comes to personal finances, it's unlikely we'd ever have a clue that they were experiencing woes similar to ours. Why? As a means of reiteration, it's because a person, particularly a man, is more likely to confide ANYTHING else in his neighbor beside the fact that he is struggling with money issues.

Call it a macho thing or whatever you will, but it's true, guys hold money matters much more near and dear to the heart than women. And *that* is a bad thing. We'd sooner confess a drug addiction or other indiscretions than ever *hint* we're getting calls from bill collectors.

In the late 1950's and early 1960's credit cards became the newest tool of the economic revolution in this country. It took some time, but eventually caught on around the globe. Trillions of dollars are spent each year on the *buy now, pay later* plan.

And even though it has become quite the international way of life, we have systematically erected quite an impenetrable fortress, a *plastic prison*, behind whose walls many millions now sadly reside.

This book promises to help you get yourself out of debt. If you follow the guidelines closely you will be on the road to recovery almost immediately.

You must keep in mind that (in most cases) you didn't get into debt overnight, so you must also understand that you won't be out of debt tomorrow. It will require some dedication, focus and assertiveness, but as soon as you start putting these proven methods into practice there will be a sense of the elephant finally removing his foot from your chest.

Stop me when the situation sounds at all familiar.

"I've been working for the same company for thirteen years and even though I had plenty of seniority, the cutbacks at the plant included a reduction in my salary."

Or - "I used to get a ton of overtime. Not any more."

Or - "Our mortgage payment had to be increased significantly because they didn't take out enough for escrow. That extra amount is choking us!"

Or - "Who ever figured I'd miss *this much work* as a result of the accident?"

Or - "My maternity pay could only take us so far. I had to stay home for the baby!"

Or - "Downsizing...I hate that word!"

Or - "When they said *no payments till next year*, well, I guess time sure has a way of flying!

Or - "Hey, you have to take a shot, right? I really thought that this was *the* business venture that would pan out for us!"

Or - "Before we knew it we had to pay for the kids' college educations!"

Or - "Maybe I was just plain reckless with my spending!"

WAIT! That last one is quite the admission. What a harsh, yet insightful statement. Isn't it a basic tendency to want to blame some*one* or some*thing* else for our personal shortcomings, errors in judgment or misfortunes?

Only when we are able to stop rationalizing and take full responsibility for our actions will we begin to see a light at the end of the tunnel that doesn't belong to an oncoming train.

We have, however, become such creatures of Madison Avenue habit. Think about it. When was the last time you saw any advertisement, either on television, online or inside an actual store, that didn't offer you the chance or even implore you to put your purchases on a credit card or to buy them *on time*?

Buying on TIME

That adage sure has a double meaning. It would be more accurately stated as buying "*over time*." At least that implies it will take longer to pay for your purchase than if you plunked down cold, hard cash for it. And who is to say that you will indeed pay for it "*on time*?" What if you are late once or twice or heaven forbid, more frequently? Then you aren't paying "*on* time" at all.

But placing the blame on a society whose very economic strength lies in the credit lines and limits of its citizens is downright sacrilegious. How can we hold Visa, Mastercard and their brethren accountable for our miscues, errors in judgment, or plain old poor "*fiscal fitness*?" We don't blame violent crimes on violent movies, do we? Perhaps we do, but instead of blaming any*body* or any*thing*, the rest of this self-help book will go on the premise that whatever happened to put you behind the eight ball, simply HAPPENED. And life will now go on for you.

It is time to pick up the pieces and get to work in a productive manner, one that will ultimately benefit not only you, but benefit our economy and society as a whole.

It might sound like a lofty undertaking, but I assure you it is really rather easy.

What you will learn here is regrettably not taught *throughout* the public school system, although many curricula are beginning to include the subject of personal finances.

The how and why you're where you're at financially now are no longer relevant, and no longer shall they be associated with your dilemma. From now on we'll be dealing with - *what's next?*

This is your journey to financial freedom. Strap yourself in, buckle your seatbelt, secure your life vest and be sure to keep your arms and legs inside the turning pages at all times.

You are about to embark on what may be *the* most productive ride of your life. You hold the key in your hands. Turn the page. Go ahead. Don't be afraid. Being in debt is not a crime. There is NO debtor's prison in America. The only crime, is failing to utilize the resource at your fingertips to plot your personal escape route that leads to a very joyous debt end.

One major caveat before you advance another step, however:

I'm asking you to ask yourself a very important question. "Am I in too deep mentally?" If you do not relate to any of the scenarios discussed with regard to your indebtedness but know or at least sense that your troubles have been brought on as a result of an addiction you've developed to spending on credit cards, you owe it to yourself to get in touch with Debtor's Anonymous, a support group formed in 1971 that was modeled after other successful 12-Step programs such as Alcoholics Anonymous.

Their phone number is (781) 453 2743.

Here is the address to their national headquarters:

Debtors Anonymous
P. O. Box 92088
Needham, MA 02492-0009

Or visit them online at: **www.debtorsanonymous.org**.

You can always pick this book back up at a later date, but if you aren't mentally prepared to stop charging at this point, and I mean cold turkey stopping, what you read here will be of no benefit to you; because there's no way you can get yourself out of debt while adding more fuel to the fire – in the form of more bills to your steadily growing stack.

Chapter 3
MY KINGDOM FOR A BUDGET

The hackneyed expression "the lifestyle you've become accustomed to" means nothing with respect to personal budgeting. No matter your social position, regardless of the amount of money you are capable of bringing home and forgetting your potential for increased earnings, **EVERYONE** needs to structure and live within a viable and realistic budget; the emphasis being on "realistic."

One of the major contributing factors for slipping into deeper debt is our negligence in this area. We rationalize, saying we aren't kindergarteners any more, what's the point?

I submit to you a spin on an old saying. You might be familiar with "the *cart* came before the *horse*," but in the case of the credit industry it was more a matter of "the *card* coming before the *course*!"

If only they would have taught us personal finances back in grammar school. If only we would have talked about bank accounts in middle school. If only they would have considered putting Budgeting 101 on the curriculum in high school before we went out into the big bad world of college and beyond.

Perhaps then, the number of folks up over their ears in debt today would be significantly lower than 70 Million. Perhaps not!

Prevention is the key to lowering susceptibility to disease and the same can be said relative to debt. If we are forewarned as to the various pitfalls we can expect to encounter, debt is, to a large degree, preventable.

Share this part of the book with your kids. I don't care if they are still pre-school aged. In fact, better still if they are. As soon as our children learn to put full sentences together and understand full sentences we utter to them, it's soon enough to talk to them about personal finances.

Why? Why talk about money in front of the kids? Because every study conducted on the subject concludes that the number one reason for divorce in this country is a couple's inability to deal with personal financial matters. And undoubtedly, when the subject comes up and occasional bouts of shouting are overheard, *the children already know anyway*.

Put on your sweats and get focused. Its time for a little exercise: Gather every single member of the immediate family in the kitchen and provide each with a writing instrument and some paper. If you're single or a couple with no children do the same.

NOW...make a list and from the top to the bottom itemize all your monthly living expenses, prioritizing as you go. No hints from me here. You have fifteen minutes. And...GO!

While you are frantically going about your business, I will sit here patiently, knowing full well that everyone involved in this experiment is bound to leave at least three items off their list. And I can sit here knowing this as a result of over 25 years experience seated opposite individuals and families who've provided me with their own *"complete"* lists.

Finished?

Now, from left to right, starting with Mom, because ladies always go first, everyone take a turn reading your list out loud.

None of the participants has exactly the same items on their list do they? Even if they do, chances are they're not in the same order of priority.

Even being as close to a situation as a spouse or child may be, there are still elements of each list that one or the other or *none* of you has put down. And **THAT** is why **EVERYONE** needs to live within a budget!

Priorities are a funny thing. One person's meat is another person's potato. But the meat and potatoes of every budget, the number one item of concern must be the rent or mortgage. It's really quite simple; if you miss your rent or mortgage payment you can literally be thrown out in the street. While it is true that this would leave your creditors in a bit of a quandary as to where to send your statements, that's not the way you want to get around dealing with them.

Let's carry out the theme of prioritization. After the rent or mortgage payment and any home maintenance or condominium association fees come the utilities. The good news is you've managed to make another rent or mortgage payment, but if your electricity or gas gets shut off for non-payment you're back in a world of hurt.

Some items on your budget are negotiable, you can cut certain corners here and there, but when it comes to the energy that runs the house there is no margin for error. Sure, there are plenty of ways to use fuel economically, and, depending on the system you have in place at your home, these cost-saving tips are available through your local electric, gas or water companies. Some will even average out your utilities over the year so each payment is the same, and that's helpful to a degree.

But we are talking brass tacks here, making sure your power is **NEVER** interrupted. And when I say this is not a negotiable item, here's why.

Example: You just received February's heating bill. It comes to $340.00. Unfortunately, money is tighter than usual and you can only send $170.00. Guess what? The power company, having let you skate for a few week's worth of delinquency in the past, pays a visit to your house (usually while you are away at work) and cuts off not half, but your **ENTIRE** power.

Most power and water companies aren't at all vicious, and do allow more slack than the above example provides; but for the sake of making my point I had to take a minor liberty.

So please power companies, don't send me cards or letters extolling your virtues. I *have* seen a number of situations where clients have rather unceremoniously suffered "power kill" and it was no easy task getting reconnected.

Any item that will take away your creature comforts, your shelter from the cold (and in February in places like the North and Midwest it can get awfully chilly) has to be considered a *major* priority.

Next on the priority parade is food. You would be surprised to find, as I used to be, that most people forget to include this life-sustaining item on their first list; considering it more as an afterthought. What a *terribly costly mistake* that is!

Food might even place a fraction higher along the practicality chain. Let me see, if I don't eat I get sick. If I get sick I can't work. If I can't work I don't get paid. If I don't get paid I can't even pay my mortgage; not to mention all the medical bills that would start rolling in.

So, take stock in your food costs. How much money do you spend to make sure the cupboard isn't bare? And how much goes to paying for lunches every day? If you are good, really good, and can brown bag it on weekdays, you've got a leg up on most of us. But if you must *buy* lunches, be sure to include an accurate figure in your weekly budget.

Then, multiply the amount times 4.3, because that is precisely how many weeks there are in each month. Every third month contains a fifth week. If you don't account for it, your budget will never balance.

Editorial note:

"America, proud as she is, remains the largest debtor nation on the face of the Earth. It is more than a tad hypocritical to preach fiscal responsibility in the face of practicing utter fiscal irresponsibility."

Next in line are usually the car payment or payments and their accompanying costs, such as gasoline and insurance. I say usually because most cities, at least most small cities, do not have mass transit and therefore rely on personal transportation on a daily basis, like the family car or truck. And at today's gasoline prices - that expense IS major.

If you are **NOT** one of those people, then you must determine your monthly commuting costs, whether they're for car pool, bus, taxi, subway, train, tram, boat, airplane, helicopter, hang glider, parasail, rickshaw, mule or horseback.

If you can come up with an alternative mode of transportation you use that is not included in the aforementioned, please send me a memo.

Do you shop around for gasoline? For auto insurance? You should. Like interest rates on credit cards, practically all fixed expenses are negotiable items. We'll be dissecting that strategy a little further on down the road.

So…you've got the roof over your head, your utilities are all present and accounted for, enough food in your stomach to sustain you and your ability to get to and from work all figured into your monthly budget. Excellent! But here's where things begin to be a little less cut and dried, and more diccy gray areas arise as far as priorities are concerned.

One notion not yet mentioned, and for many this item comes right off the top, is tithing. To be brutally honest, I know of just a few families that tithe, therefore, in the grand scheme of things, since we are dealing primarily with the public in general terms, this category was not among my top five. But you know who you are, and your religious conviction is certainly strong enough reason to place tithing at the top of your budget. Far be it for me or anyone else to question tithing as a major appropriation of your family's funds.

You'll notice things get grayer from here on.

Alimony and Child Support: An ex-spouse would be rather disturbed to learn that this monthly obligation is considered quite so far down your priority totem pole. I feel it's very safe to say that in *her* or on rare occasion *his* mind, there's breathing - with alimony and child support running a very close second.

I am an advocate of being a responsible parent and living up to one's family financial obligations, particularly when it is for the welfare of our children. I do not tithe, but after breathing, my first thought had always been for the benefit and well being of my son. That's just the way it was and always will be.

Maybe I've just related with a few more of you with that admission. Good!

Continuing: What about Child Care, School Costs, Medicine, Clothing, Club or Union Dues, Lawn Care, Pool Service or Cable TV? We can't forget our computer cable modem or Internet Service Provider. I'll leave these up to you to arrange in order of greatest personal importance.

What about Beauty Shop or Barbershop visits? We have to sport a well groomed appearance in order to feel professionally comfortable among our peers and co-workers. Where does that category fall in your budget?

Student Loans: We used to "forget" those. But since the Federal Government began turning student loans over to public sector collection agencies, those obligations have managed to make their way quickly from our back to our front burner.

The standard rationale given for not repaying student loans is that regardless of your major, scholastic endeavor or ultimate GPA, your present career simply does not directly tie into your chosen field of study. Therefore it didn't serve its intended purpose. Therefore you feel less obligated to pay it back.

What you are doing in essence, by failing to pay back your student loan is effectively putting a damper on possible funding for prospective students, who, like you, might only be able to further their education with the financial assistance of Uncle Sam. That's something to think about before skipping a payment to your Guaranteed Student Loan (GSL) lender.

Interesting side note here:

While with CCC, Dad and I paid a visit to the head honcho of student loans in Washington, DC back in the mid-eighties, for the express purpose of trying to get the government to refer those *misguided* or *forgetful* former students to us for help. You will be as shocked to hear the response we got out of that high-ranking official as we were when we heard it.

He looked us straight in the eye when we said we'd send payments directly to the government for NO FEE, that we would realize our financial support from the other *non-referring debtors* that those students had, and that no fees would be charged to the students...and said "We don't need that. We'll just add the collection agency fee to their balance right off the top!" For all your help, Mr. G-man, thank you, thank you very much! We two Elvises just had to leave the building after that pretzel logic. However, that visit taught us to make sure we at least brought that obligation to the attention of our clients with kids and to those younger clients that had outstanding student loans.

Hobbies: This is one area that can usually be trimmed down quite a bit, particularly if you are paying for cigarettes or alcohol consumption on a regular basis. It is easy for a non-smoker and non-drinker to flatly tell someone "Just quit!" That statement is more difficult to adhere to than the famous Nike ® slogan "Just Do It ™!"

Physical fitness is not easy to achieve and neither is sound "fiscal fitness." I can tell you that if you are working diligently to pare your budget and live within your means and it begins to fray your last nerve...this is not a good time to try the cold-turkey approach to ending any other addiction.

I am reminded of the time a middle-age couple sat across from me to discuss their personal financial *mess*, to be blunt. It started out innocently enough, but when we finished listing all of their fixed monthly expenses and began talking about structuring a repayment plan to their creditors all heck broke loose.

"What about the booze?" she asked.

"What booze?" he said with firm denial in his tone.

I really think the question caught him off guard, particularly when they were opening up their *financial lives* to a person who, until moments ago, was a total stranger. One can only imagine what kind of coercing it took to get him to honor the appointment she most likely made on their behalf.

Maybe he wasn't expecting to have to confront *other personal issues* during this visit. Whatever the case may have been, the air of uneasiness that filled the room felt like we were mired in rush hour traffic behind a diesel fuel spewing semi.

One thing led to another and I, with limited experience in dealing with feuding couples, attempted to intervene. "Um…since the so called cat is now out of the bag, lets just see what we can do to include a reasonable figure for that item in the family budget," I chimed.

Then and there I realized just how important this item can be. Apparently the gentleman had recently cut his intake back to a bottle of scotch *every other day* as opposed to his prior One-A-Day (not to be confused with the famous vitamin) regimen.

Now, it doesn't take a CPA to determine that if you are spending in the neighborhood of $20.00 a day, nipping *"Scotland's Finest"* as my client put it, you are living in a lush subdivision.

However, suggesting to someone who's been imbibing the same scotch for ten years that they might try switching to a cheaper brand produces the same results as, say, sprinkling the ashes of a dear friend off the front end of a speedboat. It comes back at you in a worse way.

These examples were offered up as devil's advocate scenarios. Because no matter how much I have taken the "norm" into consideration and regardless of the extensive time I've toiled in the credit, collections and counseling fields that led me to my formula, there will be those that feel my *prioritization* of budgeted expenses is way out of whack.

For every single item in your budget there can be reasons why *this* might be higher on the list than *that*. They're entirely up to you.

Having said all that; on the following page is a "typical" budget. If you fill in the blanks where the dollar amounts are intended to go it should help you out a great deal.

I know, I could have just printed the list for you at the top of this chapter, but then you'd have missed the reasoning behind prioritization.

OUR FIXED MONTHLY LIVING EXPENSES

(And those items that can be reduced in order to make ends meet)

Mortgage Payment or Rent... $_____

2nd or 3rd Mortgage or Equity Loan.............................. $_____

Utilities, including Electric, Water, Gas & Phone............ $_____

Food Costs. Home and Away..................................... $_____

Condominium or Homeowner's Fees......................... $_____

Vehicle Payment/s... $_____

Insurances, including Auto, Home & Health.................. $_____

Other Transportations Costs (Tolls, Car Pool, etc.).......... $_____

Alimony, Child Support.. $_____

Student Loan Repayment.. $_____

Child Care, Including Day Care, Nursery, After Care...... $_____

Regular Medication.. $_____

Laundry, Dry Cleaning.. $_____

Club or Union Dues.. $_____

Home Maintenance (Lawn Care, Pool Service, Other).... $_____

Cable TV, Internet Service Provider, Satellite................. $_____

Subscriptions – Newspapers, Mags, CDs & Books......... $_____

Beauty Shop, Barbershop... $_____

Alcohol & Tobacco... $_____

Entertainment & Hobbies or Crafts............................... $_____

TOTAL FIXED MONTHLY LIVING EXPENSES............$_____

If you have expenses that are NOT mentioned in this chart, make sure you add them to your own list or your total will not be accurate.

Once you've determined your TOTAL FIXED MONTHLY LIVING EXPENSES you are ready to approach your creditors with a plan of repayment in accordance with the next chapter.

Chapter 4
TALKING CAN BE GOOD,
BUT ALWAYS GET IT IN WRITING!

For those of you who are "in deep" there's a very good chance that this chapter will help you the most. It tackles the important matter of how to talk about your bills with strangers…or how NOT to talk to them, depending on your set of circumstances.

They can call themselves account representatives, accounts control analysts, recovery agents, customer relations personnel, financial account associates or anything else they choose, but the truth is they are, at first, total strangers.

We are able to draw certain first impressions whenever we converse with an individual for the first time, aren't we? Maybe the person is off-putting, aggressive by nature, cold, blunt, loud, annoying, pretentious, boastful, over zealous, has an attitude that rubs us the wrong way, and, on occasion, is just plain nasty.

The stranger I'm talking about here will be called a *bill collector* from now on, to make it easier to identify him or her. Besides, none of us goes home and tells our spouse "Honey, I had a call from an *accounts control analyst* this afternoon!" No, we say "I just got off the phone with a (@~!*&$!!#! bill collector!"

The essential ingredient for cultivating meaningful negotiations with your creditors is establishing proper and thoroughly diplomatic communications.

You must immediately and forever eliminate the (@~!*&$!!#!s from your vocabulary. It won't be as difficult as you think once you finish this chapter.

Let me put it a different way. If you must talk to these guys you've got to learn the right approach! Talking about bills, even with a spouse, family member or close friend is hard enough; so when the bill collector comes calling, we immediately hunch our backs in catlike fashion, ready to pounce as soon as their first *disturbing word* is uttered. And that disturbing word from the bill collector is usually "*hello!*"

Most people get into debt innocently enough and the thought of being treated like the kind of debtor who just runs willy-nilly over his creditors, the classic deadbeat if you will, is anguish inducing.

But you must temper that anguish with a calm, almost reserved demeanor if you wish to make your important points during your discussion. The moment you lose your temper, your credibility is gone and quickly behind that follows your overall confidence.

It is safe to presume that the moment you fall 30 days behind on any of your accounts you will receive a letter, and on the heels of that letter, a follow-up telephone call should be expected. Your awareness of this inevitability will serve to put your mind at ease right away. You won't be *surprised* to hear from your creditors or at least you won't have to *act surprised* when you do.

When I was a kid my Dad owned a collection agency. Don't think for a second that a lot of what I heard around that office didn't make a big impression on me.

His agency was well respected, a prestigious service in fact, and back then, even though there weren't laws on the books protecting the debtor; and his collectors were mild-mannered compared to others in the city. I heard some real horror stories.

Here are a few:

Long before the FDCPA came into existence (in-depth coverage of that legislation later) bill collectors went to any and all lengths in pursuit of the almighty "balance in full!" They didn't stop short of threatening imprisonment, repossession or generally predicting awful things happening to those who failed to meet their financial obligations; kind of like Harry Brown, Bill Kruglak and The Cicero Gang of pages past.

And the "balance in full" was sought right away for one simple reason, and that reason still applies to this day:

The faster an agency bill collector recovers the money from you, the greater the commission he or she earns.

That is why the most aggressive call you'll get is likely the first one.

If it isn't too late, if you haven't yet received that first letter or telephone call but you see the writing on the wall and know that very soon you will lag behind, it is a great idea to be the one initiating first contact with your creditors.

Think about that for a second. Instead of you being put on the defensive right off the bat, you are putting yourself instantly in control, because your call will come as a major surprise to your creditor and catching *them* off guard versus them catching *you* off guard can bolster your position.

It also speaks volumes to the notion that you clearly have a finger on the pulse of your personal finances and are prepared to deal with them in a professional and dignified manner.

Now I'm guessing, but the percentage of instances where the *creditor* takes the first step towards contacting the *debtor* instead of vice-versa is 99.45%...or $1/100^{th}$ of a percent greater than the claim of purity by **Ivory Soap** TM®. It just isn't done.

We would rather delay the inevitable and risk facing consequences wholly unprepared. Then, ignorance or temporary insanity is the defense we're likely to invoke.

You should start with a simple telephone call. Always use the toll-free number provided on your monthly statement; save money. It shouldn't cost you anything to make an inquiry or discuss your accounts with any of your creditors.

Sometimes a simple phone call isn't that simple. You may have to go through a maze of recorded menus, but be patient. Now is NOT the time to start losing your cool.

When you finally have the chance to speak with an actual human being, you'll want to appear relaxed, calm and in total control. If you let the connection process disturb you it will be reflected in the tone of voice you bring to the conversation and that will not benefit you in the least.

There are departments too numerous to mention within the structure of the typical credit card company. Your first goal is to speak with someone who has actual contact with your account. There may be a screening process, since most credit card companies and banks shelter their collection staff from incoming calls…*even when you are returning their call*, oddly enough. They are what I term "overly autonomous."

Somewhere between 1950 and today that "personal touch" faded from the landscape of American business, and attention to real customer service has remarkably and sadly all but disappeared.

That's okay...deal with it. Resign yourself to the notion that you are merely a number prior to your first discussion. After "making contact" that should change, and you can see to it that it does.

One thing I cannot stress enough: **Always write down and save the name and direct telephone number of the person with whom you speak!** That is a cardinal rule that allows for NO exceptions. This will cut down some of the steps and frustration the next time you communicate with them.

Chances are your account is not yet in the Collection Department...that usually occurs the moment you become 60 days past due. So, at any stage of delinquency prior to 60 days, you'll want to ask to speak with someone in the Credit Department.

If you are further along than 60 days you already know who's trying to reach you, so there's no guesswork involved there; it's the Collection Department. This, you will soon learn, surprisingly enough, might even be in your favor.

Here's one tip that you should never lose sight of:

No matter how frustrated you might become, avoid using profanity!

Oh sure, you say, you knew that. But there are times when we are so blown away by what the person on the other end of the line is saying that we stray from Webster's and summon vocabulary we never knew we were capable of using.

Profane language paints an instant negative picture of you in the mind's eye of the representative with whom you are conversing. It says - here is an individual that is incapable of expressing him or herself professionally, someone who is frustrated and someone whose word should be doubted. And it buries you in a hole out of which you may never fully climb.

Choose profound over profane and be victorious in each phone call.

Your best bet is to engage in the 3-F approach - Firm, Friendly and Factual dialogue and NEVER use the 4th F word. Keep in mind how your hackles raise when you hear *their* voice. Now, imagine the shoe being on the other foot...your tone should become serene. The news you are about to give them is not what they want to hear, but it is news they would eventually learn anyway.

The number one concern of any lender or credit card company can never be understated or reiterated enough; it's their BOTTOM LINE. Therefore you want to get to the point quickly *and* offer a resolution all in this first call. You want to express deep concern over your present financial situation and at the same time offer them a viable payback plan.

You want to avoid lengthy sob stories. Believe me, they've heard ALL of them before...even stories you think YOU made up. This is YOUR first time experiencing this four-letter word called D-E-B-T. They deal with it 24/7 *nearly* 365.

Here is an example of how your conversation might begin. You may wish to sprinkle in a few of your own words; however, key words that should be included will be in **bold, *italicized*** print.

"**Hello, my name is** _____ do you have my account pulled up in front of you?"

Even if they do not have your record handy and even if you've provided your account number for what seems to have been twenty times, offer it again politely.

Continuing... "And ***what is your name please***?" (Write it down NOW!)

If they are unwilling to give you their last name for what they call "security purposes" (which is really for THEIR security or to cover their butts if someone pursues legal action) ask them for their operator number and say you are only inquiring in the event you may need to get back to them in the future. You shouldn't get too many objections to that request.

This early into your conversation you can get an idea of the personality with which you're dealing. From barely audible to eardrum splitting the bill collector's vocal style runs the gamut.

Accept the entire range of vocalization, even if the sound makes you want to crawl through the wire and strangle them. Control, remember? At all times and at all costs...*you* must remain in control!

Continuing..."*I just wanted to let you know that I* (exchange "I" for "we" if appropriate) *have come upon difficult times and am unable to send the minimum required payment on my account. I do take my financial obligations seriously, which is why I took the initiative to contact you, and I've come up with a plan for repayment that I know I can handle.*"

You need to have done your homework up to this point.

You want to offer a realistic plan based on your ability to pay.

You can only do that by taking the figure that is your TOTAL FIXED MONTHLY LIVING EXPENSES and subtracting it from your TOTAL MONTHLY INCOME.

Here's a very quick example:

Your fixed expenses are $3000.00 and your net income (take home pay) is $3450.00. You therefore have $450.00 to apply to your discretionary or credit obligations.

If you offer too much, out of fear of reprisal or for whatever reason, you are committing a grave error. Next month when your payment is due and you can't send it because you overestimated your ability – you're no longer to be believed, and that could make future dealings all the more difficult.

Take stock in your personal budget. Determine how much money you can realistically send your creditors...all of your creditors, every single month without fail. Then and only then can you have the kind of conversation suggested here.

Assuming you've figured out a realistic payment, let's get back to some elements that belong in that first conversation.

Since you've taken the initiative here, your call should not sour, at least not this early on.

One thing you should know going in: For the most part, the individual you have your first conversation with is likely unable to accommodate your request for a lowered monthly payment. This is primarily due to the fact that he or she is someone who fields hundreds of calls each day and has to make a determination as to where your call must be routed.

Don't let this discourage you. So what...so you have to repeat your story *all over again!* Remain poised and focused. *You know how much you can afford to pay each one of your creditors and you will accomplish your goal!*

Eventually you will be talking to a person who *can* help you, and, depending entirely on the extent of your delinquency and previous communications with them, they very likely will try to work things out with you.

If your stage of delinquency is extremely past due, contrary to what you might think, it will be easier to strike up a deal because they'll have waited so long by this time that **any money received** is like a bonus from their perspective.

Congratulations!

You just hung up the phone (you didn't slam it down either) and are well on your way to debt free living. Can it possibly be that easy? When it comes to phone etiquette, actually, **YES!**

There are a few things I don't feel I can stress enough that will help you, so in some cases I'll stress them a second and maybe a third time. The following is one such instance.

Every time you speak with someone you must always remember to write down the date and time of the call and the name of the party to whom you were speaking. That bears repeating:

<u>Every time you speak with someone you must always remember to write down the date and time of the call and the name of the party to whom you were speaking!</u>

But you can't stop at this point. Immediately after you've taken down the aforementioned details grab a pen or sit down at the computer and compose a letter similar to the one found on the next page.

PROPOSED PAYMENT LETTER

Date

XYZ Credit Corporation
2000 Way Serious Interest Way
Anywhere, USA   Zip Code

Attention: Mr. or Mrs. Dunning

Dear Mr. or Mrs. Dunning,

   It was very nice speaking with you this afternoon. I want to thank you for understanding my financial situation and your company for agreeing to work with me in my effort to eventually pay off my XYZ Credit Corporation balance.

   Per our discussion, I will be sending you $____ on the _____ of every month until such time that I am able to increase the payment.

   I am hopeful that my setback is only temporary and I assure you that I, more than anyone else, am anxious to see the day when I no longer owe XYZ Credit Corporation money.

   Meanwhile, if you need to contact me, please do so either by mail or by calling me at home after 6PM Monday through Friday; as I am not allowed to receive personal calls at my place of work.

   Thank you for your consideration and assistance.

Sincerely,

_____

Let's pick that letter apart line by line.

The **DATE** is important for two reasons.

1. The person to whom you spoke will have you and your situation fresh in their mind when they receive this letter; because you are going to spend about three bucks to send it certified, return receipt requested through your local post office.

2. Just in case! Just in case down the line someone denies you were the one to make initial contact. You are basically covering yourself, that's all.

If you've never sent a certified letter before, it's not a daunting task. Your postmaster or local post office teller will show you what needs to be done.

The reason you want to send it certified, requesting a returned receipt is for you records. Proof, if you will. You will have the signature of the person you sent your letter to...unless some other person in their mailroom happens to sign for it. No matter what, though, someone WILL sign for it and you've got a name associated with the date it was sent - and that's key to this exercise.

Critical Note: Whenever you send *any correspondence* through the U.S. Mail to your creditors, do it in this fashion. It is amazing what leverage you create by keeping accurate records. It is equally amazing how quickly you'll lose control of the situation *without accurate records.* I'm not a big fan of email for this step even though you can do it so much more quickly; however, acceptance of an email does not officially constitute the same kind of acceptance that a certified and actual handwritten signature does.

The **COMPANY ADDRESS BLOCK** should be accurate and filled in completely in order to expect your party to ever see your letter.

Possibly the most important part of your letter, body text not withstanding, is the ***DEAR*** _____ part. Knowing the name of the person you spoke with and then addressing them personally gives you a most positive psychological edge for several reasons.

People like getting mail, and they like the old-fashioned kind that you have to open with your hands, unlike email. We don't particularly like to get bills, but aside from *that* kind of mail, people like to know that others are thinking about them...no matter what they may be thinking.

You will impress them, especially if you *spell their name correctly,* and, at the same time you are placing the onus on them to now **DO SOMETHING**.

Additionally, it tells your bill collector that you pay attention to detail (whether *they* realize it psychologically or not) and if you remember their name, their guess is that you will live up to the terms of the repayment plan you've structured.

By now you have to be thinking I was right, that you can actually get yourself out of debt. Forget about cursing the day you signed on with a credit counselor or considered "hiring" one. The best thing you can do is resign yourself to the fact that they may have provided you with a sound service at the time when you most needed their intervention. I've never said credit counseling agencies aren't good for you, I've only said you don't NEED them.

I would equally encourage you to take a few mechanics classes or suggest you bone up on computer science so that the next time you need to fix your car or PC you'll save money too. The true credit counselor in me is always looking for the most economic solutions for my clients; and as a reader of this book I feel that qualifies you as one of my clients!

There is much to be said about having established working relationships with over 15,000 national creditors and developing a reputation over a quarter of a century in the service industry, however, you can not have any of my qualifications and still be in the position of taking complete control of your personal finances by yourself with the tool you are holding in your hands right now.

I want you to benefit tremendously from my field experience. There really Is far less of a need for credit counseling agencies than ever before and the beautiful thing is - **Creditors are finally**

realizing that the smarter approach is to deal directly with their customers.

Sure, there are those hardcore debtors who will never pay the money they owe, regardless of the extent of their knowledge, but for those "deadbeats" - let's just say this book is not for them. They are probably sending away for get rich quick pamphlets, eager to make that one big "killing" that will whisk them off to early retirement on the sun-baked beaches of a Pacific Island somewhere.

It never ceases to make me chuckle when I see those infomercials hosted by supposed self-made millionaires, hawking real estate deals and selling bank foreclosure lists.

The saddest part of it all is that the general public really believes they can be on the next program, appearing before the whole of planet Earth as yet another one of Joe Real Estate Mogul's success stories - as a member of the new Millionaire's Club. In actuality, a couple of those hucksters very well might have sold a house or two in their day...*but all their real money is coming directly from the sale of their audio and video tapes to pie-in-the-sky believers, like you!*

You have to learn to become a resister to ward off such come on efforts. You need to be resolute; you must do the research and expend the necessary mental and physical energy it takes to ensure your personal success in dealing with your creditors. The same rule applies to whatever situation you might find yourself; professional, personal or spiritual.

I use real estate get-rich-quick schemes as a parallel example to my response to the question about "what can you do for me that I can't do for myself?" to bring things into clearer focus. In much the same way individuals will fail miserably in their efforts to get rich quick, so too will those looking for an easy way out - fail to get themselves out of debt.

Returning to our letter:

The **BODY** language is important. And I don't mean what kind of chair you sit in to write it, but the words you choose when trying to make salient points or win your creditors over to your side.

You want to avoid being too flowery or too dramatic. Remembering that they've "heard it all before" will serve you well whenever you put pen to paper. It isn't really necessary to share personal tragedies with your creditors, even though your situation might have arisen as a result of one.

You be the judge here. If you feel as though the person you spoke with might be a sympathetic individual, based on something they might have shared with you in your conversation, then by all means if you are so compelled, share some of your relevant personal details with them.

We are all pretty good judges of human character and characters, aren't we? We can tell if we have someone's ear or if no matter what we say we can sense the non-committal dead air on the other end of the phone.

Be sensible in your approach and let your first impression weigh heaviest on your decision to either let a total stranger into your personal life or not. Your only real connection to them is the bill *you* owe. Don't forget that!

A simple "we have fallen on hard financial times" should be sufficient in most cases.

If you **DO NOT WISH TO BE CONTACTED** in any way, shape or form at work, you must tell them so IN WRITING! If you SAY you told someone that over the phone it won't carry any weight. If you SAY anything, it can always be disputed, met with contention or out and out denied. **And, it is another great reason for sending all your mail certified, requesting a returned receipt**. The federal law regarding this is quite clear and will be touched on in the chapter regarding debtor-creditor legislation.

Finally, **YOUR ATTITUDE** in signing off is a strong reflection on you and may mean the difference between their working with you or not! By telling them you are very concerned about your debt and expressing that you have every intention to meet your obligation to them you are providing reassurance, and reassuring your creditors is appreciated more than you can imagine.

Then, sign your name and seal the letter. Before long, you can count on hearing from them again.

That's just one type of letter. There are many others that will help you accomplish different smaller goals as you blaze your path toward debt-free living.

Did you know that you might be able to *reduce or even eliminate interest* on your accounts?

Did you know that under very extreme and specific circumstances your creditors are willing to *completely eliminate your entire balance* as a hardship?

With the power of reasonable negotiation in your trick bag you can truly dictate your own destiny, and that doesn't merely hold true when talking about personal finances.

How often have you "gotten your way" in discussions? Do you recall the give and take, the ebb and flow of those negotiations? Whether you succeeded or failed, the road that produced the ultimate result should be memorable. **Learn from your losses and be humbled by your victories.** That attitude will definitely lead to future successful negotiations.

I cannot provide you with one certain method of negotiating, because no one method works on or for all people. You can have the identical situation with two different credit card companies and if you employ the same negotiating methodology chances are fairly even that you will get split results. Of course, chances are you will meet with two negative results or two positive results too.

There are some things that hold true no matter the company, no matter their representative, no matter the size of your balance, no matter how far past due you are. And here they are:

Even if it hurts so badly you want to cry, always treat the person on the other end of the phone with respect. But do so without appearing phony. Always stay focused on your goal...a negotiated arrangement that you know you can handle. And always, always be truthful. The truth can always be retold...lies are too hard to keep track of.

If you have more than just a couple of outstanding bills, it is possible for conversations to run together. Let's say in a fit of what you feel is brilliantly spontaneous thinking you come up with a real doozey of a story for your delinquency. Great, but rest assured the bill collector is going to make a detailed note of it. When he or she calls you back next week, your story better not change too dramatically or your goose is thoroughly cooked as far as expecting to carry out further negotiations in a smooth and easy fashion is concerned.

That is why I advocate telling the truth, and telling it all the time!

Telling the truth worked for me. I have heard lies before, as one of the dreaded bill collectors discussed earlier. Lies don't work. The truth does! From holding the ogre's side of the telephone and hearing "it all" hundreds of times over, I can tell you that it does not take a Rhodes Scholar to see through the smoke.

On the other hand, I was always more sympathetic (I wasn't in debt when I was a collector so I couldn't have been empathetic) when a person said: "Hey look, I am really in a bind and I don't know what to do," or "I'd really like to pay you but I just don't have any money right now!"

At least I could differentiate between debtor types. The honest debtors who just fell from grace were as easy to spot as the plotting, fibbing BS artists whose intention was to stall and stall and eventually skip town without making restitution of any kind.

There are the in-betweens too; those who grasp at straws just to fend off the wolves and might try a little sleight of phone until they get busted. But for the most part there are two types of debtors: Those that will pay and those that will not.

Once you're pegged as one that will not, you instantly attain the dubious distinction of being associated with that infamous group, known in collection circles as **THE DEADBEATS.**

It is one of those first impression deals that you will not be able to shake for as long as your debt is outstanding. It's like failing a test and then struggling for the rest of the semester to try to make up percentage points for your overall grade; only worse - because unlike a semester of school that lasts a few short months, **your credit history follows you around for life.**

The preponderance of industry professionals agree that the very best way for debtors to communicate with them is through the letter writing process. Therefore, this chapter, from this point forward will focus on situations that crop up similar to yours and the proper templates you can tailor to your specific financial situation.

As a side comment, the way my Dad became involved in the credit counseling business was as a result of his efforts to help a friend get out of debt. He did this personally, not under the guise of any company offering assistance; rather, he negotiated with his friend's creditors based on his experience in the collection *game*.

To make a long story short, he was able to save his friend thousands of dollars merely through verbal negotiations. Over the years I've refined his groundbreaking approach and established this effective letter writing process that has helped many people; some you might even hear from if you read the back cover.

The letters that are contained in this book are culled from a combined 75 years experience in the credit, collections and counseling fields and should benefit you tremendously as there are several different categories. One of them or a combination of several should hit home for you.

Let's Talk About Settlements

There may come a time when your luck changes for the better. You may not feel that way now as you're going through your difficult times, but in this life things do seem to run in cycles, so, maybe you're due for something positive to happen regarding your fiscal condition.

That isn't to say that someone finally flew over your house in a hot-air balloon and dropped a giant sack filled with hundred dollar bills that just happened to land on the big red target you painted there years ago, nor did Uncle Sam decide out of the blue that you overpaid your fair share of taxes since you were a teenager, nor did you win MegaMillions or anything quite THAT miraculous; but something on a less grand scale might have occurred that did put a respectable chunk of change in your pocket.

For this example's sake, let's presume you now have that small inheritance or minor windfall.

What is the best approach to take with found money? That answer changes like the wind. Everyone's needs are different. Spiritual need outweighs financial needs for some, even if they are behind that eight ball and up to their scalp in debt.

Do we put the money to practical use and pay down some of our debts or do we use it to take a much needed vacation? On the surface that sounds like a relative no-brainer, but really consider the latter over the former, if for only a moment.

I'm not trying to make a case for you to say chuck it all and hit the road, but there are two diametrically opposed schools of thought here.

Could it be that a vacation is just what the doctor ordered to help you restore your rapidly flagging sense of sanity? Would a week or two in the country listening to birdies chirping and sipping water from a pure brook be such a terrible alternative?

Isn't it possible that recharging your batteries by getting away from it all might be curative?

I contend that if the timing is right, maybe you just ought to take that break from reality that could be achieved by a vacation.

But the key word here is "timing!" If the money you came upon doesn't make a dent, doesn't scratch the surface of paying off a good portion of your obligations - it might be the best remedy of all to breathe that country air for a while, so that when you come back to your reality you'll be ready to immerse yourself back into finding a solution to your money problems and have a clearer head to tackle matters.

Should your decision be to take that vacation - you can rest assured your creditors will still be there when you return, waiting to hear from you or trying to get in touch with you. Once they do, I wouldn't confess to drinking mimosas on a private beach in Tahiti. News that you just returned from the lake fishing and camping won't sit too well with the bill collector that works on commission and probably hasn't seen a beach in decades either!

It is alright to wrestle with what to do with the money. It might not be the best idea to throw it all at your bills.

Thinking things through thoroughly is the best thing you can do. You have to weigh all sides of the issue and make a calculated decision based on whichever side tips the balance of the scales; even if it's only ever so slightly.

In the event you opt to make payments to your creditors, you have to construct a plan. You must know the amount you wish to propose as SETTLEMENT IN FULL of your obligation to each creditor you contact. You will need to put together a written settlement proposal that is clear, concise, **fairly realistic** (I'll touch on that a little later in this chapter) and totally feasible for YOU.

Depending on your previous experience with your creditors, negotiating settlements might be a lot easier than you may first think. If your creditors can't stand you because you've always given them "attitude" whenever they've spoken with you in the past, it could be something that is virtually impossible to accomplish.

Assuming that you haven't said nor done anything to your creditors that has made their "representatives" hurl Nerf ® darts at a picture hanging on one of the walls of their partitioned cubbyhole that they pretend is you, I'll proceed with the concept of the SETTLEMENT LETTER.

This presumed scenario has you coming into several thousand dollars, and also presupposes that the amount won't come close to paying ALL of your actual balances IN FULL.

While it may take two or three times the amount you've managed to obtain to entirely liquidate your debt without offering a settlement, you still have quite a powerful leveraging tool. As the saying goes, "Money talks and Poop de Toro walks."

Before when you were plodding along, barely making minimum payments or not making them at all, your creditors were used to it. They were used to seeing tiny payments when they trickled in, and that, in their unedited opinion was a wonderful thing...because the rate of interest you were paying (which is also negotiable and will be discussed later too) is high enough that even making your minimums ensures them that you will be on their books for a very, very long time.

And while you would never guess, based on the calls you've received from their collection staffs, your creditors actually "prefer" you draw out payment over, say, **your lifetime and the lifetime of several generations that follow you.**

PLEASE NOTE: All of the letters you write should follow the same formatting prior to the salutation as does the first letter.

SETTLEMENT IN FULL REQUEST LETTER

Dear _____,

I've recently received funds that should allow me the opportunity to pay off some of my obligations. I've decided to take the high road and do whatever I can to eliminate as many of my debts as possible, instead of using the money in, perhaps, less productive ways.

Presently, my balance with your company is $_____. I would like you to consider settling my account #_____ IN FULL for a one-time payment of $_____, which represents 50% of my outstanding balance.

I am proposing settlements to all of my creditors, since the amount of money I received will not serve to cover payment in full to all of them; and instead of choosing one creditor over another I thought it would be fairest to make the same overture to everyone involved.

Please feel free to call me at home after ___PM (or wherever and whenever is best for you). My phone number is _____.

Should you accept my proposed settlement kindly indicate as much in writing to _____ (your full address goes here). Once I am in receipt of that documentation I will immediately forward the funds to your offices.

Please include in your letter to me that the amount of $_____ will pay my _____ (their company name) account IN FULL and that you will be furnishing that information to the credit bureau to which you report my account.

Thank you for your consideration. I look forward to hearing from you.

Sincerely,

_____

The question begging to be asked now is this: Is it reasonable to think your creditors will be willing to accept a settlement IN FULL for ½ their balance?

The answer is - IT DEPENDS. Sometimes they might accept settlements for LESS THAN ½ their balance. Sometimes you won't get as big a discount. It's a bit like Priceline ® or Travelocity ® where you don't know unless you put in your bid.

In this case, the further past due you are the better your chances of effectuating a smaller settlement; because your creditors are used to receiving hit and miss payments; if any payments at all. And at this particular juncture they'd likely take whatever they can get.

However, if you have been making regular monthly minimum payments - they would be less inclined to grant a 50% settlement; simply because up until this point you'd never presented yourself to them as a financial risk. Therefore, and quite ironically, if you've been a good payer it can hurt you in this effort. Not funny, I know.

If you fall into the first category, I'd say your chances at making a 50% settlement are, appropriately, 50-50. But you never know unless you ask; so go for the moon and if you end up negotiating a 75% or 80% settlement - that still represents a sizeable savings to you.

Some years back a knot in the settlement system was tied, so that now, if you make a settlement with your creditor, what they may end up doing is writing the difference off as an uncollectible or bad debt. This is done for their tax purposes and certainly not for the sake of how your credit bureau reports might be adversely affected.

The snag this presents is that the government takes a look at the amount you saved by making the settlement and automatically reports that figure as taxable income…no lie! So, you are likely to end up paying tax on the deal after all is said and done.

It sounds to me like that's the same Uncle Sam who hangs around the racetrack or the sports book in Vegas, Atlantic City, and Branson or wherever; to be sure you sign your name to any big ticket winnings.

And, funny enough, it's the same Uncle Sam that is conspicuously absent when you toss your ten bucks a week into the Lotto pool at the office and don't win squat. He's your partner when YOU make money, but he's the cat who says "Benn who?" if I drop a chunk at the Blackjack table, or **sell a few million copies of my book!**

That's fine, I'll pay THAT tax. My sentiment of "Thanks for Buying This Book" is polar opposite to that of Abby Hoffman of antiestablishment Chicago 7 fame who once wrote a book titled "Steal This Book." Many people did, incidentally!

I hope you bought mine!

It is entirely up to you to determine if the savings you realize from the settlement is worth all the effort. Even if you negotiate what ultimately ends up being a 30 to 50% discount, it would probably be worth it. I doubt it would be worthwhile at a rate much lower than 30%, though.

The absolute most important aspect of the SETTLEMENT LETTER is the **PAID IN FULL** part. Unless your creditor is willing to accept this offer under that condition, forget it, period and exclamation point! You do not want to find yourself running into a situation where you've exhausted your funds, assumed you've paid your balances off entirely - and then get a phone call or a letter in two weeks asking for the balance!

A few pages back I spoke of the hardship scenario whereby the creditor might be willing to eliminate all or most of a debt.

The next letter would be the one to write if you fall under this category of debtor:

HARDSHIP LETTER (Non-Medical)

Dear_____,

    I regret my situation is such that I have not been able to make any payments to my creditors for quite a long time.

    When I was first granted credit by your company I was in a much more stable financial situation. I am sure you will find that my record of payment has always been excellent, however, things have changed dramatically for me over the past_____ (timeframe) to where I am now on a fixed income, bringing home only $_____ per month in social security and disability benefits.

    My rent is $_____ and my electricity averages $_____each month, which, as you can see, barely leaves me any money for personal essentials such as food.

    I realize this is a very big request, but I would like you to consider writing off my balance as a hardship. I cannot at this point in time see any possible way of paying you back. I have exhausted whatever options were once available to me.

    Should you decide to honor my request it would relieve a tremendous burden I have been forced to carry around with me for so long.

    In the event you are unable to zero out my balance as a hardship, I will understand, but the fact remains I simply cannot make payments; a sad fact I'm saddled with having to apprise all of my creditors and various other places where I owe money.

    Thank you for your consideration and for the privilege that having your credit represented to me back in _____ (fill in the date) when I first opened an account with your company.

Sincerely,

_____

Don't expect to pull a fast one with this letter if it doesn't truly fit your financial profile or circumstances because your creditors know far more about you, your earning power and potential and "private" accounts than you wish they did.

You will not be able to con your way into any deals like this. And you need to know that this book was written to HELP you, not to give you any notions that are in the least bit underhanded. If you follow the intent of this information *you will get yourself out of debt.* Should you freelance and become too creative for your own good it very likely will come back to bite you in the keister.

I live by the axiom "cheaters never prosper" as opposed to the infamous W. C. Fields statement: "A thing worth having is a thing worth cheating for!" If you are an Abby Hoffman or W. C. Fields fan you'll be disappointed to learn that I have little in common with either of them.

Keep in mind; you will not be able to convince anyone that you are destitute without producing proof that you receive SSI benefits, food stamps or other documents to support your claim of poverty. So if you aren't "that" bad off, don't make your situation "appear" any worse than it really is. Trust me on that advice; it will save you certain anguish in the long run.

If you DO fall under this very specific category, rest assured one thing; in all the years I've either dictated or actually written this letter on behalf of a client - it has met a 100% success rate; provided, of course, that the information was verifiable.

The next letter coming up, I'm sorry to say, won't have nearly the success rate as the one above, although I think it should. It too is specific in nature and can probably be written by a much larger segment of the debtor population.

It deals with medical debt as opposed to credit debt, and to me there's a massive difference between the two.

Believe it or not, even in this day and age, there are still people in America that don't own a single credit card; yet they are deeply in debt as a result of either lingering medical bills as a result of the amounts not covered by insurance, or from not having proper, if any, medical insurance to start with. You might recall the Bill and Cindy Roberts story earlier on.

In editorial fashion, here is my heartfelt thinking on the subject:

It's not exactly like you rang up your internist and said "Hey, doc, I have a few hours to kill before I go back to the office today. Could you fit me in for a quick appendectomy?"

Or like you dialed your neighborhood nephrology lab and said, "It's a rainy day and I really don't have anything else to do, so can you hook a brother up to your dialysis machine for a few hours?"

My intent is not to be flippant or the least bit sarcastic with these comments, only a tad humorous. After all, if there isn't a little bit of levity attached to this subject, dry as it can be, the potential of boring you to tears, if not to death, is pretty strong!

This may sound irreverent now, but the point I'm trying to make is that the medical struggle itself is hard enough to deal with, without having the financial aftermath to compound the memory and misery of it all.

And NOBODY "plans" to have surgical procedures, at least not like the ones I mentioned. We don't bargain for stacks of medical bills, yet for some unforeseen and forsaken reason we get them.

And when we cannot pay them, and wind up having to talk to bill collectors about them, especially ones like George whom I spoke of before, it is foreign to us. It is complicated all the more when we've never used credit cards and do not have a clue as to how vicious efforts can be to try to pry money out of our wallets, our bank accounts or by any other means.

Some debtors suffering from an abundance of medical bills are unwitting souls lined up perfectly in the crosshairs of those scavengers who wouldn't think twice about taking advantage of them in their time of financial woe.

A case in point and one that is not at all extreme, one that I've personally attested to on numerous occasions, is the tale of the recent widow or widower in his or her seventies that happened to amass thousands of dollars in medical bills as a result of the passing of their spouse; thereby turning the survivor into the heir apparent to the debt as a result of signing on as the guarantor during the insuring process.

Neither septuagenarian ever had to deal with finances above and beyond their fixed monthly living expenses; simply because when they were in their teens and early twenties…THERE WERE NO SUCH THINGS AS CREDIT CARDS!

The world still managed somehow to rotate on its axis then, as incredible as that may seem.

With the newly inherited debt came the obligatory and shocking first contact from their medical practitioner's office. Even to the wiliest senior, they've not had to endure a contact like this in their lifetime, and, unfortunately, they end up making whatever promise they *think* the "representative" wants to hear - because they are scared out of their wits.

Intense fear then sets in because they realize they've made a commitment that they know is impossible to uphold. They stay up practically all night worrying about how to make things right and then out of nowhere (actually they're everywhere late at night) a commercial by a local lender pops up on their TV screen promising to make life wonderful once again if only they'd take out an equity-based mortgage on their home.

Now there are times when this kind of loan is practical, sensible, even intelligent, but this is NOT one of those times.

Why tie up the proceeds of the home you've worked a lifetime to pay off in order to pay back medical expenses you never bargained for in the first place?

I simply cannot get my head around that one any more than I could ever, with a clear conscience, recommend someone in their advancing years take out such a loan.

The real kicker in all of this is the interest rate, which undoubtedly will be quite elevated - because the lender knows people in their eighties aren't going to sign a 30-year fixed mortgage, even if they were offered one. People in their seventies and eighties, for some uncanny reason I choose to call *intelligence*, know that the likelihood of them reaching the ripe age of 110 or 115 is rather slim.

I wouldn't be an advocate of a flex-loan or any other loan that is set to escalate in payment size over X amount of years or one that carries one of those looming lead balloon payments after a short period of time either.

Nor would I suggest that anyone at an advanced stage of life take out a "small" loan from a loan shark (I mean loan company) because the interest alone will eat them alive (speaking of sharks) and will probably devour the surviving members of their family for a couple of generations to follow.

Alright, that's a bit exaggerated, but you get my drift. I just don't see EVER borrowing money to pay off medical bills when you're an advancing senior citizen.

IMPORTANT CAUTION!

NEVER BE CONVINCED TO BORROW MONEY TO PAY A MEDICAL BILL WHEN YOU ARE AN ADVANCING SENIOR CITIZEN!

You should be receiving total medical coverage provided 100% by this country if for no other reason than to **THANK YOU** for all you've done to contribute to our society in your lifetime. I truly believe that.

I apply that same school of thought to younger folks too, but when you are not living on a fixed government stipend that barely pays the rent, food or utility bills - the story is similar to a degree, but different in enough ways to warrant making some restitution.

The scariest thought is that someone, regardless of their age, would actually take out an interest-bearing loan to pay bills that do not carry interest charges.

That used to be a statement one could meet without reprisal, but many states have passed legislation that allows the physician, the hospital, the dentist, the ophthalmologist, etc. to bill upwards of 7% interest on their medical bills.

As always, check your state laws to determine how you will be directly affected.

Write the next letter if and only if your situation is one that warrants it. It is a letter to your doctor/s requesting they zero out your balance as a hardship and is quite specific in nature.

Again, if it doesn't apply to you **DO NOT USE IT!**

HARDSHIP LETTER (Medical)

Dear Dr. _____, (Use I or We where appropriate)

In all my years I've managed to live a debt free life. When credit cards became popular I still felt I would do better to live within my means, paying cash for the things I really needed and waiting until I could afford some of what could only be called luxury items.

I'm sharing this with you prior to asking you a favor that will certainly help ease my stress and concern and hopefully serve to help me get healthy quicker.

Dr. _____, I am living on a fixed monthly income (here you'll want to briefly explain from what source your income is derived – be honest) of $_____. That amount barely stretches far enough to pay our necessities each month.

I appreciate the medical services and follow up attention you provided and feel you should be paid. I also understand that a large portion of your bill was covered through our Medicare/health insurance/HMO (or by whatever means it was in your specific case).

The amount that remains unpaid is a terrible burden on me and my family. I have tried to send you payments, but I'm sure you've noticed you haven't received any money since _____.

The favor we're asking is that you zero out the remaining balance; either as a professional courtesy or as the financial hardship that it represents to us. It makes no sense for me to promise payment to you when I know there is no possible means with which to do so.

If you would kindly consider my request and get back to me I would greatly appreciate it.

Sincerely,

_____

You don't have to be in your eighties to send the above letter, and you can tweak it to fit your situation, but the basis of it has to be the fact that you have no other obligations and you haven't the resources to begin or to continue making payments.

The older you are the better your chances of having the balances completely expunged, for the obvious reason that there will be more of an understanding with respect to the fixed income section.

However, provided you keep it legit, regardless of your age, there's a good chance you'll touch a chord in your doctors - that chord that hopefully had them entering med school and its profession in the first place; the chord of compassion.

There may come a point when you know the length of time you'll need in order to get back on track with your payments.

There is an upside to that from the creditor's standpoint, and that is that they know you're on top of your situation and aren't preparing a nonsense excuse to carry you over the next few months.

They don't really want to play that "caught you in a lie" game any more than you want to. In the case where you know how much time you need it is appropriate to fill in the blanks and send the following letter to each of your creditors:

MORATORIUM REQUEST LETTER

Dear _____,

    I am writing you today to request a _____-days moratorium from my debt with you. My financial situation, while not allowing me at present to remit payments to you, is about to change for the better.

    Starting on the ___ of _____ I'll be in the position of resuming and perhaps even increasing payments on my account.

    In the meantime I'm asking that you freeze the interest on my account during this ____-days timeframe.

    This will allow me to focus on my job, my family life and all of my fixed living obligations, which in turn will carry me stress-free to my payment resumption date.

    Kindly respond to my moratorium request in writing at your earliest convenience.

Sincerely,

_____

Whether you receive a positive, negative or no response at all to this letter, it makes sense to send it.

If they say YES, mission accomplished. Go about the next 90 or however many days you requested with the full intention of living up to your promise for the next payment.

Should one, two or all of them be indignant and flat out say NO to the idea, at least they'll know that you're in control of your finances and might be a little less likely to give you attitude or aggravation during that timeframe.

The same positive result will apply if they don't get back to you at all. Remember, you are sending this letter just like every other one – requesting a certified return receipt. Somebody somewhere will receive it and you can refer to it the next time they contact you.

I've always felt that NOT TALKING to your creditors is the best of all worlds, provided you've established a written agreement with them regarding repayment and not calling you.

The next letter is one that we sent from our counseling agency on behalf of ALL of our clients, and even though we had written agreements with the major credit card issuers and retailers as well as Visa and Mastercard, it is something you might be surprised you can accomplish on your own.

If you are making regular payments and your balance is failing to drop in the least, you NEED to send this letter. With the optimal results you could be looking at saving hundreds or even thousands of dollars over the duration of the repayment plan you've established.

This letter might be your first follow-up letter after you've structured your repayment program as well.

After several months of remittances you'll call on them to give you interest relief too, but you don't want to press that issue too soon.

Show them you're living up to your end of the bargain for at least six months and then put this next letter to use, altering the wording to fit your situation; as this one is for those that have been making consistent payments and have not entered into an alternative payback arrangement.

REQUEST INTEREST ELIMINATION LETTER

Dear _____,

    I think you will agree that I have been a good customer for quite a long period of time and that I am making regular monthly payments with rare exception.

    It has gotten to the point where even though I am making payments, nothing seems to be coming off the balance and it feels like I'm merely spinning my wheels in my attempt to get this balance paid down.

    From this point forward I'd like to request that you eliminate interest on my account, so that everything that I send goes toward the principle balance.

    My debt has grown so frustrating and is creating great hardship with respect to my ability to meet my fixed monthly living expenses. If the money I was sending at least made a sizeable dent in the balance I'd be able to rationalize directing future payments your way.

    Of course I appreciate the credit you've extended to me, but ask that you work with me now so eventually this account will be marked *Paid in Full*.

    Please consider my request and get back to me at your earliest convenience.

Sincerely,

_____

This isn't the end of the letters; more are inserted in subsequent chapters.

Chapter 5
MORE ABOUT BANKRUPTCY

B A N K R U P T C Y ~ it IS just a word you know. But try telling *that* to someone facing the very real prospect of having to file it - and you've got a whole different ballgame on your hands.

Up to this point I've discussed some of the psychology of bankruptcy. In this chapter I'll hit the nuts and bolts connected to the filing process.

Even though deciding to go through the actual process weighs heavily on most debtors' minds, it is a relatively painless procedure. When handled properly, and by professionals who work in the field every day, filing personal bankruptcy can be as freeing as anything you may ever experience.

I would never recommend anyone file bankruptcy by her or himself. Yes, there are kits you can buy for about $25.00 that provide the forms to fill out, but I always defer to the pros whenever I'm dealing with something rather foreign to me. Kind of like the "let a mechanic fix my car" mantra to which I strictly adhere.

That is why *I hired an attorney* when I filed bankruptcy. Even though I am as well versed as anyone when it comes to the credit industry and debtor-creditor law in general terms, I did not want to leave anything to chance. Besides, when the time comes to stand in front of the bankruptcy trustee it's real nice to have someone at your side, holding your hand in the proverbial, if not literal sense.

How do I know I should file bankruptcy? The answer is simpler than you would suspect. All the indicators are there, you just need to see the forest for the trees.

If you are one of the honest debtors, your financial dilemma didn't just happen yesterday. It was a gradual process, one that has had you agonizing over a period of time, maybe even a few years; and making the ultimate leap is the only thing standing in the way of restoring your sanity. And I do not say that merely in jest.

I'm not big on statistics, which is why I rarely give answers with numbers in them in interviews...heeding the words "statistics are used like the drunk uses the lamp post, for support, not illumination" and the other more well-known "figures lie and liars figure"- but I do know, from more than a passing interest in the field, that many, many people have committed the ultimate personally destructive act of suicide as a direct result of their inability to deal with the pressures caused by money problems.

They did not know that bankruptcy was available to them. They may have thought that only companies go bankrupt.

Whatever their deeply rooted reason, they chose a way out that I pray you never even consider.

No matter how bad your financial picture looks, it isn't THAT BAD!

On the flip side other readers will stop me in my tracks and say: "What's the big deal about bankruptcy?

Well it is a BIG deal. It is a serious situation and the decision to file should come about thoughtfully and with a measure of consternation.

Those who might take the procedure lightly will learn later on that there is a certain stigma attached to it. I cannot in good conscience state that everything will be just like it was before you filed - because that would be less than realistic.

Bankruptcy should be a legal means of finding financial relief and should not be considered until you've tried every other means possible to repay your *"debts to society!"*

For decades it seems, Congress had been working on legislation that would severely restrict an individual's ability to file personal and corporate bankruptcy, and, to reiterate; it passed the **Bankruptcy Abuse Prevention & Consumer Protection Act of 2005** (BAPCPA) which severely restricts ones ability to file personal bankruptcy.

The Act went into full force and effect on October 17, 2005 and became necessary because so many people were taking advantage of the old laws by squeezing through carefully thought out loopholes in the system.

This meant that those who wound up ultimately paying the price for the cheater, as always, were you and me, the taxpayer.

One of the key components of the Act is that no one is allowed to file personal bankruptcy without first contacting and then passing an accredited program of credit counseling.

How ironic for yours truly, three years after walking away from what was turning into a derisive and deceptive industry Congress was now making it mandatory for consumers to show certification of program completion from a credit counseling agency in order to be able to file bankruptcy.

I guess you could say this book beats the whole system to the punch. Naturally, lawyers and other "bankruptcy credit counselors" will be perturbed to learn that not only aren't credit counselors necessary appendages to YOUR financial equation, neither are bankruptcy attorneys – in most instances.

And what I will assure you is that neither has any compunction about charging you money for their services...the services you do not need if you follow the processes in this book closely and carefully.

With the Act, whereas at one point in time you could simply run up a gigantic debt load and decide when the bills start flooding in to go belly up - it no longer works that way.

You cannot even "offend" your creditors by running that charge to the max trick; because the BAPCPA, imposed by the Federal Government, is geared to stop you in those tracks.

There are situations where the only possible choice to make is filing personal bankruptcy.

Let's forget the dishonest fiend who will figure out a way to beat the new system anyway, and get back to you, a debtor that feels very close to the end of your own rope.

If you read the title of the BAPCPA word for word it clearly explains its intent.

However, there are considerations beyond the monetary ones. There are the psychological ramifications it may have on you. There are interpersonal relationships to think about.

If you are married to someone who has never used credit and has managed to do well without it, you are dealing with a whole different kettle of fish than the spouse who is a present or former credit user or abuser.

You'll want to consider rather deeply what kind of issues filing bankruptcy will bring to your marriage.

Your family life is paramount, but what will the knowledge of your bankruptcy do to your professional relationships?

Will it impact your friendships?

It is easy to say: "If it has a negative impact on my friendships then they weren't friends to begin with!"

Or "My co-workers can't hold the fact that I filed bankruptcy against me!"

But believe me, down the road a bit *those issues do arise* and you should have some idea of how you're going to deal with them.

According to Mary Trimble, author of the American Bar Association's booklet "Dealing with Debt" from their Practical Law Series ~ **"Bankruptcy is a legal remedy for people and businesses who need a fresh start when faced with insurmountable financial difficulties. It is an undertaking with serious consequences in terms of future access to credit. A record of the bankruptcy stays on your credit report for 10 years. <u>So it is important to consider all your options before filing for bankruptcy.</u>"**

And **THAT** is precisely what we will have accomplished by the time this chapter is concluded.

I have seen people file bankruptcy for hundreds of thousands of dollars and three months later they're deemed credit worthy. WHY? Because they earn half a million dollars a year and *they have no financial obligations* to speak of after their bankruptcy is discharged. Don't think creditors aren't monitoring your earning power very closely, even after you file bankruptcy.

You're **ALWAYS** a prospect. Remember that! You are considered an excellent risk almost immediately if you are bringing down that kind of yearly income. And, from their perspective at that point in time, it makes perfect sense to view you in such a bright and shiny new light.

But woe unto you if you are barely grinding out twenty-five grand, are struggling to raise three kids and pay the heating bill by the time old man winter rolls around! It hardly seems fair, but it is logical.

The poor guy or gal, who is creating 100 different meal ideas out of pasta, ends up paying exorbitant rates of interest while Joe Slick in his brand new Range Rover is being offered lines of credit, second mortgages, and every other enticement you can imagine that will get him or her back on the creditors' books.

In ways, you can see where it's all a silly little game.

The haves continue to have, and the have nots continue to hope they pick the right six lottery numbers twice weekly at the end of their "essentials" food shop. It is one of life's cruel jokes. Have a quick laugh and forget about it.

Bankruptcy is a relative issue. It became a relative of mine in 1996...a relative I won't soon be inviting over the house for dinner soon or one I'll be offering shelter to on a cold winter's evening either. In my case, filing personal bankruptcy happened to be a necessary evil and something I thought long and hard about before doing. Even though the handwriting was on the wall, I delayed the inevitable longer than I probably should have, but I had my reasons.

There are two basic forms of bankruptcy that individuals can file. Either Chapter 7, which is the total liquidation of your debts or Chapter 13 which is the court ordered liquidation of your debts (detailed in just a bit).

Here are a few items that are exempt from bankruptcy.

- *Your House or Real Estate*
- *Personal Property ~ Such as household goods, jewelry & clothing*
- *Cash*
- *Retirement Funds*
- *Your take home pay/net income*

You do not have to surrender any of the preceding items under Chapter 7 of The United States Bankruptcy Code.

Where things tend to get tricky and sticky is when you take it upon yourself to make large cash advances on accounts *less than six months prior to your bankruptcy filing date.* When the court appointed trustee sees these items a red flag goes up and he or she might have a sense that your intent from the outset was to defraud your creditors. That would not only be a bad thing, it likely would prevent your bankruptcy from being adjudicated.

At the beginning stages of this writing there were 36 states that had their own exemption laws and 14 that gave the option of choosing either State or Federal laws. I do not have the list at my fingertips, but you can find out what the law is in your state by placing a call to your State Attorney's office, speaking with a local bankruptcy attorney, or performing a little due diligence online.

The aforementioned exemptions vary from state to state, so don't assume those listed are exempt in YOUR state.

Another thing to consider: Bankruptcy, ironically, is not a cheap procedure.

Think about it...here you are, in debt up to the hair follicles on your scalp, and on the scene now appears a representative of the legal community bearing news that he/she intends to extract some dead presidents from your wallet. I mean, talk about adding injury to insult!

But you will get what you pay for!

Scene 1 ~

A dude walks up to you on the street and says: "Hey man, wanna buy a Rolex?" He pulls up his sleeve and reveals two-dozen of them, offering them for twenty bucks apiece.

Scene 2 ~

You walk into a renowned jewelry store. Under glass and a trillion watts of direct spot lighting are two-dozen Rolex watches, offered at approximately 400 times more than our street "vendor."

Me? Oh, I'd probably star in **Scene 1**, making my purchase outdoors. I might even have managed to knock his price down to twelve or fifteen bucks.

But here's the roughly $9,975.00 question:

What are the odds that my **Scene 1** timepiece stops working before the little hand passes the twelve a second time?

Conversely, the odds of *you* expiring before the real Rolex does are probably a lot higher. I guess I've made my point about getting what we pay for.

That isn't to say you can't shop around for your bankruptcy attorney, in fact, I encourage you to do that. Any attorney worth their salt will happily disclose their qualifications and experience, unless their sheepskin is of some bogus variety. If you are really skinned it might not be a bad idea to consult an attorney at a Legal Aid office in your community. Just keep your eyes open, do your homework and you'll be fine.

I happened to file Chapter 7. I had to, because there was no possible way for me to begin making restitution. **And that is the time when you know Chapter 7 is right for you.** The amount owed was way beyond my ability to even begin a repayment program. I did reaffirm on one debt, however, meaning I elected to repay it - to the tune of $1000.00 over a two-year period.

I had some guilty feelings about the amount they made available to me which I had fully accessed, and because I had enjoyed such a longstanding and mutually satisfying working relationship with that particular creditor, I wanted them to really know that my filing bankruptcy was something I *had to do* as a result of a specific situation beyond my control or means of determining beforehand.

I really appreciated their being there for me and I couldn't turn my back on them entirely. And you know...I feel better having repaid at least a tiny portion of what I owed them. And now, 15 years later, once again...I know why Howard Ruff felt the way he did back on *The Oprah Winfrey Show* when he revealed that he too had to file bankruptcy; which would make him #61 on my list. And the circle makes another full revolution!

Typically, from the start of the process to the finish, Chapter 7 bankruptcy filings take between four and six months, (mine took just under four months) - unless your situation gets into a heated battle between you and your creditors based on improprieties in which they feel you might have become engaged.

In that case you could be in court for a couple of years trying to finalize things.

Chapter 13 of the United States Bankruptcy Code is the personal debtor's equivalent to the filing of Chapter 11 by corporations. It is essentially court ordered liquidation but is considered "reorganization" because your bills are all paid.

Your creditors will each receive a small portion (usually in the 5 to 10% range) of their original outstanding balances, according to the court, and in most cases, interest is eliminated in order to allow you to reach your day of financial freedom.

When you seek assistance from and complete a debt repayment program through a licensed credit-counseling agency, most credit bureaus regard that in similar fashion to filing Chapter 13. You are rated an R-7, which is a designation meaning that you "made or are in the process of making regular payments through a wage earner or similar plan."

I discuss those ratings in greater depth in Chapter 9.

It usually takes between 36 and 60 months to complete repayment under Chapter 13 and for the most part you can keep all of your assets, including your house and car, even as the proceedings are taking place.

You are NOT eligible for filing Chapter 13 if you owe over $250,000.00 in unsecured debts, such as credit cards, personal lines of credit, etc. Neither are you eligible for Chapter 13 if you have in excess of $750,000.00 in secured debts, such as your home, equity credit lines, etc.

All things being equal, assuming you qualify for either Chapters 7 or 13, **the major difference is that with Chapter 7 you wash your hands of all your debts and immediately are operating with a clean slate.**

Chapter 13 takes a longer period of time; however, you ARE paying back your debts to the court's satisfaction. No need for confusion; usually your situation will determine which Chapter you should file.

What are the advantages and disadvantages of filing one form of bankruptcy over the other?

I know of only two first-hand examples: Mine, and that of a close personal friend. Sure, I had seen a handful of clients who had to file bankruptcy because they got to the point where they no longer could maintain a repayment program through credit counseling, but first-hand is always best, so I will share my feelings as well as the overall ramifications the process had on yours truly.

Since my bankruptcy was discharged the road hasn't been quite as rocky as I first thought. I haven't been granted any credit cards, but I haven't tried getting any either. I have received countless offers for credit cards that you pay for; the ones that are accompanied by outlandish interest rates and up front fees required to establish your line of credit.

So far I have managed to steer clear of all of them. If it weren't for the strength and resolve of my wife, had I been alone in this world of credit, I would most likely have taken at least one or two of them up on their offers. Of course, I would THEN, undoubtedly, have found myself *"alone in this world of credit!"* And how could I have blamed her!

Going through the rigors of the bankruptcy process, even though they may have excellent credit, still wears on the spouse just by virtue of being married to you.

It is a pretty awesome feeling not having the mental pressure of worrying about "who gets what" every day.

UPDATE: Circa 2003

I subsequently re-established my credit and enjoy a high rating at the credit reporting agencies. This time around, though, I try to pay my balance in full each and every month. My creditor would prefer I "take my time" but I learned a valuable lesson and am practicing what I am preaching. Later on I'll show you how to get your credit back once you've gotten yourself out of debt; so stay tuned!

My buddy filed Chapter 13. We have discussions from time to time about the issue. He consulted with me prior to filing, seeking my feedback, knowing my background and the fact that I took the Chapter 7 plunge about a year earlier.

His situation varied from mine in that he was in a business partnership with his brother, and certain major equipment purchases for their shop were guaranteed by my friend's signature alone. Failing to meet those obligations would impact their business and certainly their brotherly relationship; and those factors, as well as others, precluded him from filing Chapter 7.

There are moments when we both regret our decisions to file. But there are more moments when we realize that had we not, we'd probably both have suffered heart attacks from all the stress attached to our situations.

Don't let stress over unpaid bills be the cause of YOUR death.

Oh, it **CAN** cause your death. Clearly that would be the ultimate way out of your bills, but it is **NEVER** necessary.

I cannot recollect all the stories I've read online, in the newspaper or seen on TV where a person leaves a suicide note, citing his or her inability to cope with their finances as the major cause for ending their lives.

It leaves a sickening feeling in the pit of my stomach, because I know it *never* has to happen. If you are teetering - it is important for you to know that unless you change your outlook, your outlook will change you, and not for the better. Believe that!

There are two other choices when all is said and done. Either you pay your bills back eventually, or you don't.

REMEMBER!

THERE IS NO DEBTOR'S PRISON IN AMERICA...PERIOD!

DON'T KILL YOURSELF OVER YOUR BILLS!

Perhaps the above message would have been a more appropriate title for this book!

When you sit down and realistically look at your financial picture, if it turns out that it's a struggle just to put food on your table, it is time to file some form of personal bankruptcy.

Go directly to an attorney who specializes in the procedure, do not PASS GO, do not pay a bill collector a single dollar, seek your relief and don't stop until you find it!

Once your ship comes in, you can always reaffirm. And you better believe your creditors will be willing to take money from you – even decades after the fact.

Chapter 6
THE INFOMERCIALIZATION OF AMERICA

It all started in the early 60's. My recollection of the Pocket Fisherman® the Veg-A-Matic® that dices and slices, the Ginsu Steak Knives® and the Bamboo Steamer® all serve to date me somewhat, but they were the precursors to today's infomercial explosion.

We would always get a kick out of those *commercials*, as they were once called, and, while I never knew *anyone* who ever purchased a single one of the aforementioned products, we ALL knew their slogans word for word.

And it's funny how cyclical things tend to be. We entered the 21st Century being bombarded in unprecedented fashion by products flashing across our TV screens at the speed of light, and, unbelievably, a decade later the pace has quickened. We are so inundated it is sometimes hard to tell the difference between a thirty minute infomercial and a thirty minute sitcom.

In fact, some infomercials are so funny; they deserve Emmys ® for Best Comedy Show in the TV Sales category.

A while back I had a hard time falling asleep. That inability gave birth to this chapter, for as I laid there on my couch channel surfing, it seemed as though every other station had some kind of paid advertisement.

So I paid closer attention and turned it into a personal study. The results were astonishing.

Out of the 71 stations I received at the time, 32 were airing infomercials! Can you believe it? Okay, it *was* ten minutes after three in the morning, but still…45% of them?

Exaggerating you say?

Fine, here they are; you asked for it.

The following are not in order of preference, they are in the order that they appeared on my screen as I was feverishly clicking my remote. It would not surprise me if most of them have long since been erased from America's stream of consciousness.

Just so I don't have to type them in each time, after every product you see, pretend there's a ® or a © or a ™ after them, please.

ProActive – A zit cream, basically. We all know how important looks are to everything in life, right? Puberty should have been left off the list of things we have to go through on our way to maturity.

Psychic Friends Network – Man, if I had a nickel for every time I landed on *that* infomercial I would print, publish and offer this book FREE to everyone. But I don't, so please pay full price for it. Believe it or not, I have worked with the Head Psychic lady personally…before she carved out her incredibly profitable career. I wonder if she knew she would make so much money from that project. Of course she did! SHE'S PSYCHIC!

Wireless Marketing – This must be one of the newer ones. It's new to me anyway. Here's their deal. They are going to PAY US to give away gift certificates for FREE satellite television dishes. We can set up our own sales force and display stands, and…wait a second, who's paying for this then? Ah, never mind, that isn't important.

The FTF Fat Reducer – Nobody wants to be fat, just like nobody wants to be in debt. These folks promise to naturally knock the pounds off our chubby bodies, making us well again. If only they could guarantee worthwhile personalities that made us interesting and non-judgmental too.

HSN and QVC – They'd probably detest my putting them together since they are archrivals, but they *are* both networks that hawk wares 24 hours a day, seven days a week and when all other channels finally go to bed they are still there to entertain and entice us. I never bought their "not available anywhere else" claims, though. Their usage of ***never before and never again*** is a little tough to swallow, especially when you can walk into your local K-Mart and have many of the same products practically smack you in the face at the cash register.

The Rotisserie Grill & Automatic Pasta Machine – He's back. Paul Popeil, the man who was the forerunner of infomercials with his Pocket Fisherman and Veg-A-Matic has returned to bring us some incredibly inventive machinery that will lead us down a healthier, more nutritious pathway; with the exception of his spray-on hairpiece. They're terrific utensils that deflect fats right out of our diets. Can't wait for his **Chocolate Ice Cream & Baked Goods Calorie Eliminator** to come out.

TAhealth.com – What could possibly be more significant than trimming down our bodies, or raising our financial status than improving our sex lives? NOTHING, I tell you...NOTHING! Just one tablet of their **Viramax** in the morning and one in the evening and voila...in one to two weeks time you will be ready to star in your own adult movie. Not that the following are associated with this product, but who cares about minor side effects like, nausea, dizziness, anal leakage, depression, memory loss, headaches, vomiting, memory loss, loss of vital organ function, memory loss or memory loss? I don't care if my erection lasts longer than an entire South Florida summer - give me that toll-free number again! What was I talking about again?

Don Lapre's Secrets To Success – Okay, I admit it, string me up by my thumbs, I bought this one. Yes, I truly did. It was on the heels of filing bankruptcy, and, well, he *is* one dashing,

All-American, successful looking son of a gun, and he *was* talking right TO ME that sleepless night...and, I, uh...felt that it would help me get back on track and...it's sitting just to my left as I now type. A weird thing happened after I received my books and videotape...I had to **wake up and go to work** if I didn't want the bank to come and padlock my house for non-payment.

One of these days I am going to go back and have a serious look at that material. It *is* a comprehensive package of stuff. My problem is finding enough time to apply its resources and make it personally worthwhile.

UPDATE: I did find and have a serious look at the material. It is no longer at my side; it has long left the premises via the trash bin. Perhaps some seagull swooped down on the dump site where it was couriered and is making a successful go of it. I hope so.

The George Foreman Grill – In his 35 years in and out of the boxing ring, George never cooked up a better plan to make money than when he attached his star to *"The lean, mean, grilling machine!"* It makes great, low-fat burgers. My son has one of these grills, and he LOVES it. Of course, my son is 5' 10" and weighs all of 145 pounds, so lean isn't exactly what he's looking for these days.

George, on the other hand, balloons upwards of 290 pounds when he isn't "training" so it appears as though the preacher isn't practicing grilling on his own utensil. Okay, so this one DID turn out to be the biggest thing since sliced bread and I'm kicking myself practically daily for not having taken stock in or hitched my wagon to THIS George two decades ago.

SMC – These are consumer products coaches. They teach us solid, realistic ways to make money. Tom Bosley (October 1, 1927 – October 19, 2010) of "Charlie's Angels" fame was the host for this particular money making alternative. If memory serves correctly, Tom hawked a few other products after this one before passing on.

BOWFLEX – This is my personal all-time favorite. "Look, I'm 41 and I'm in the best shape of my life" says the totally ripped pitchman. Right! And it all happened because of his Bowflex, and the moon is made out of green cheese and I'm Bill Gates' sole heir. The premise we have to buy into is that this chiseled Adonis got that way practically overnight, with a few simple stretches of some rubber tubes. I'm no longer "thirty something." You would have to tie my mouth shut with those rubber tubes for three months and *then* I too just might be in the "best shape of MY life!" I did buy one of these years ago, from a Schwinn dealership in town. I had it for about a year while I was living alone in an apartment. It occupied a room set aside for nothing but workout equipment. Between the treadmill, stair climber, Bowflex, rowing machine, Bullworker and chinning bar I probably had a total of a dozen complete workouts that year. When I sold my roomful of equipment, somehow, miraculously, I IMMEDIATELY felt more fiscally, if not physically fit.

Hair Club For Men – Hosted by the owner of the company's daughter these days, this infomercial and this product is probably viewed with more interest than any other. Losing hair, for men, is such a curse…at least it is seen that way by the wives or girlfriends who are "interviewed" for this show; shallow-minded as they may be. The worst thing about any hair retrieval product is their approach. "Do you SUFFER from hair loss?" NO! I have never heard anyone who's lost or is losing their hair say they SUFFERED or are SUFFERING from it. They may not be happy about the fact that it is thinning out but NO PAIN is attached to hair loss. And don't tell me the mental anguish THEY try to make you feel is SUFFERING! Take a look at the back cover of this book. You now have my opinion of how important hair on the top of a man's head really is. Nevertheless, I did buy a "piece" once. Vanity, thy name is man.

Sharper Image – I thought they were a chain of stores that featured eclectic gadgets and electronic doodads. When did they get into the infomercial biz? I guess when their Ionic Breeze machine came out, appealing to our desire to breathe healthier air and lust for general wellness.

The Internet Tool Box – Got it! It's on the other side of Don Lapre's Secrets to Success. Same deal. I haven't found the time to look at "All the Tools You Need to Master the Internet!"

But the second banana from TV's "Home Improvement" convinced me to run out and buy this Theme Ware product. After all, it does have the approval seal of the **Parent's Choice Foundation for 1997**, whoever they may be.

UPDATE: It went out the same way and on the same day as Don Lapre's Secrets to Success deal. I doubt the same seagull dug its talons into it, but you never know.

Mr. Juiceman – Wait...I LOVE THIS GUY! Jack LaLanne is well into his nineties, looks like he's in his late sixties, and has the energy of a racing greyhound. He blends his "anti-aging drink" from beets, apples, parsley and carrots. It doesn't completely stop or reverse the aging process, but it promises to slow it down. By looking at him - I'd say by close to 20 years. His mantra **"If man made it, don't eat it"** through the ages has likely made more enemies with the food manufacturers and pharmaceutical giants than even I'll make in the credit industry; for that I am appreciative!

UPDATE: Sadly, LaLanne passed away on January 23, 2011 at the age of 96 of respiratory failure due to pneumonia. Jack's principles and practices for a healthy lifestyle will live on for many generations to come. Rest in peace, Jack, and THANKS!

Free Money To Change Your Life – A geeky, nerdy, dorky, dweeby guy with thick, horn-rimmed black glasses wearing a red suit with gigantic black question marks all over it, ala "The

Riddler" from Batman fame, *was* there to show us that even we not so popular types can achieve incredible riches if we follow his plan. Bill Gates. Need I say more, Matthew Lesko? We know already, we know!

TaeBo – Billy Blanks has come up with a combination of aerobics and martial arts that has literally taken the country by storm. It is founded on the premise that exercise, a novel approach, is a good way to achieve physical fitness. Why hasn't anybody ever thought of THAT before? Buy your video and workout with the stars. Mentoring motion picture stars was never this lucrative for Mr. Blanks, and bless him…at least he is a practitioner who is in excellent shape and is doing his part to really help people feel better about themselves and their appearance…slimming them down while not making our wallets painfully thinner in the process. This one gets my thumbs up.

Rapid White Pro – Something barely believable about getting cleaner teeth that practically glow in the dark.

Exercise In A Bottle – Now here's a novel approach to…ah, forget it!

World Vision Child Sponsorship – An infomercial to embarrass American TV watchers into feeding a child (or several - for just so much per week) from a third world country. I feel totally embarrassed, but for a stronger reason still haven't sent my hard earned money toward this cause.

The United States Navy – Yes, they too have managed to submarine into the infomercial age.

Food Mover Cookbook – Richard Simmons' latest. He STILL looks overweight to me. I didn't watch it, but wonder if the product is anything like the comb-over people try prior to ordering Hair Club for Men rugs, I mean "solutions?"

Bosley Medical Hair Restoration – Not Tom Bosley, but it might as well be.

Just Kidding Video, Censored In America
The Ultimate Book of Kid Concoctions
Hook N' Hang Closet Organizer
The Red Devil Barbecue Grill
Allegro Cookware
Sun Setter Awnings
Steam Buggy
Fat Trapper
Torso Track and Torso Tiger

I grew weary and stopped adding descriptions to certain products, mostly because their names are self-explanatory, not because I wish to disrespect them.

On any given day you will find hundreds, literally hundreds of products being pushed through the airwaves. Every single "normal" commercial even affords us the opportunity to visit their web site so we can buy, buy, buy, buy, buy & BUY!

It is so easy to spend our money these days. Prior to "The Infomercialization of America" we had to waste precious time getting up, getting showered, getting dressed and getting going. Now, in milliseconds, we can stumble out of bed, drop into a chair in front of the PC and proceed to mire ourselves in a murky debt that once took at least half a day to accomplish.

We are developing into a nation of at-home shopaholics, placing wants before needs, risking our future "creditability" on the chance of having it all today.

The whole reason for this chapter is to serve as a warning:

Watching television in the middle of the night may be hazardous to your financial wellbeing.

Shopping online can be more dangerous than frequenting real stores in real shopping centers. In our never ending quest to have it all and have it all NOW, a major part of that quest is our overwhelming desire to feel better, look better and make more money; all the things they tout in their infomercials.

But when we make such impulsive purchases we lag further and further behind with our payments and become feverishly embroiled in what I call the "*video charge syndrome*."

You know how they say you should never go food shopping when you're hungry? The same rule of impulsiveness applies here.

You should never tune in to infomercials prior to retiring for the evening - because you're equally susceptible to spend recklessly by ordering online or "calling that number on your screen NOW!"

HERE'S A TIP:

If you're having a hard time falling asleep, turn on a channel that airs old black and white movies. For some reason they just make you tired by watching them. Maybe the lack of color prevents the senses from being aroused; whatever the scientific reason is, try it.

And as they say in the infomercials "It works for me, it will probably work for you too!"

Chapter 7
THERE OUGHT TO BE A LAW

There is. Actually, there are several. This chapter is for you, the honest debtor. It is here to ensure that you NEVER become a victim of abuse from bill collectors for as long as you live.

You will have enough knowledge of how to **level the playing field** by the time you finish this book; which brings to mind a golf story I like to tell.

Stevie Wonder and Tiger Woods were sitting in a bar. Tiger turned to Stevie and asked him how his singing career was going.

Wonder replied: "Not too bad, how's your golf game coming along?"

Woods said: "Not too bad, I guess. But I have been trying to iron out a few klnks in my swing lately and I...Stevie interrupts, saying: "You know, I find that whenever I have trouble with my game all I need to do is stay away from the golf course for a while and not even think about my problem and invariably the next time I go out I enjoy a better round."

"Now wait just a second," Tiger says. "You mean to tell me you play golf?"

"Sure, been an avid golfer for thirty years," Stevie boasts.

"But you're blind," Woods adds in astonishment. "How can you play golf if you're sightless?"

Stevie explains the Wonder of it all. "It's easy, really. I have my caddie stand in the middle of the fairway when I'm on the tee box and I ask him to call to me. I listen for the sound of his voice and adjust my stance to aim toward it."

"That is truly amazing," Tiger growls. "Then, when I get to where the ball landed, my caddie moves to the green or further up the fairway and the process begins again. I play to the sound of his voice," added Stevie.

"Yeah, but how do you putt?" queried Woods.

"Same principle applies to my putting. Only once I'm on the green my caddie puts his head on the ground where the cup is and calls to me; and again I aim toward the sound!"

"That's awesome, what's your handicap?" Tiger asked.

Wonder replied "Actually, I'm a scratch golfer."

"WOW, we've got to play a round together sometime," Tiger said incredulously.

"Nah, I don't know, people never take me seriously enough. Besides, if I DO play them, it has to be for money. I never compete for less than ten grand per hole" Stevie insisted.

Being one of the top players, if not *the* top player on the PGA Tour, Woods licked his chops and said:

"Okay, I'm game for THAT. When would you like to play?"

Wonder said "I don't care, YOU pick the night!"

And that is what you call leveling the playing field.

There are likely to be a few trying moments when your "normal" efforts to level matters simply aren't good enough.

No matter how you try to keep your cool under pressure, there are those bill collectors out there who are downright abusive.

KNOW THIS:

You do have rights as a consumer and they should not be a deep dark secret that can only be found with a special 3-D map and decoder ring; although aggressive, nasty collectors with rotten tactics would just as soon have it that way. After all, leveling the playing field is not what they are about. Nevertheless the laws you're about to read were meant to do just that.

Without getting overly technical I will share with you the basic principles of the Fair Debt Collection Practices Act, (FDCPA) an Act that is regulated by the FTC. Much of what follows will be excerpted from a letter dated August 1996 and issued *by the FTC.*

As previously noted, whenever I quote word for word it will be ***italicized and in boldface type.***

Here is the list of most frequently asked questions:

- ✓ What debts are covered under the Act?
- ✓ Who may collect debts from me?
- ✓ How may a debt collector get in touch with me?
- ✓ Can I stop a collector from contacting me?
- ✓ If I don't think I owe a bill can collectors still "come after me?"
- ✓ Are collectors allowed to contact my friends, family or relatives about my bills?
- ✓ Is there a late Carlin-esque list of words that collectors may not use?
- ✓ Can my creditors report my debt to a credit bureau?
- ✓ What is my recourse if I feel a collector has violated the FDCPA?
- ✓ What are some of the banned collection practices?
- ✓ Is it true if I tell someone I can't pay they can't bother me any more?
- ✓ How can I report a collector whom I feel has violated the Act?
- ✓ If I have any other questions about the FDCPA where can I go for answers?

Q. What debts are covered under the Act?

A. *Personal, family and household debts are covered under the Act. This includes money owed for the purchase of an automobile, for medical care, or for charge accounts.* That pretty much covers the entire spectrum of debt relative to John or Joan Q. Public. They could be more specific with regard to what IS NOT covered under the Act, instead of leaving gray areas as they do. Unless you are involved in forms of litigation aside from your personal debts it is safe to assume your debts are covered. If you have any question at all about a specific debt, you may write or e-mail the FTC for answers. Their contact info is provided in the answer to the final question.

Q. Who may collect debts from me?

A. On the surface this might sound trite, but it isn't. There are limits to who may collect a debt from you, limits imposed by the FTC. Only a bona fide debt collector may collect a debt from you. *A debt collector is any person, other than the creditor, who regularly collects debts owed to others. Under a 1986 amendment to the Fair Debt Collection Practices Act, this includes attorneys who collect debts on a regular basis.* In simpler terms, it has to be someone whose job is collecting debts for a living. That is to say that your creditors cannot hand over your debt for collections to some unlicensed, unregistered third party agent/thug.

Q. How may a debt collector get in touch with me?

A. *A collector may contact you in person, by mail, telephone, telegram or FAX. However, a debt collector may not contact you at unreasonable times or places, such as before 8 a.m. or after 9 p. m., unless you agree.* Now I don't personally know ANYBODY who would agree to receive frequent calls at two o'clock in the morning, do you? But those times are put in the Act for a reason, and knowing them can give you the upper hand if you've been infringed upon. *A bill collector also may not contact you at work if the collector knows that your employer disapproves.* How would the collector possibly know that your employer disapproves? You will tell him or her so and you will back it up with a certified, return receipt requested one-paragraph letter.

Remember, chances are good that the bill collector you spoke with today won't even be working at the same place the next time your account comes up for review, and no oral directive is strong enough to be binding. Once you have someone's signature, that's another story entirely,

Always back up your spoken words with written words.

Trust me when I tell you I have seen and heard it all, from skull and crossbones, tombstones, caskets and RIP scrawled on the outside of envelopes.

Postcards displaying balances with big red letters stamped on the outside declaring you **PAST DUE** are awful, but were awfully effective tactics not that many years ago.

And so were telephone calls in the middle of the night or while you just so happened to be working on an assembly line or at whatever inconvenient times you could possibly imagine. Those tools have supposedly been long since removed from the debt collector's arsenal; but to the collector that knows who the uninformed are…they'll strike without mercy.

Q. Can I stop a debt collector from contacting me?
A. *You can stop a collector from contacting you by writing a letter to the collection agency telling them to stop. Once the agency receives your letter, they may not contact you again except to say there will be no further contact. The agency may notify you if the debt collector or the creditor intends to take some specific action.* What in the world does *all that mumbo-jumbo mean?* It speaks only to collection "agencies" in this answer and leaves a lot open for debate. What about collectors from the originating creditor, may they still contact you if you write them a letter advising them not to do so? The answer I've always been given was a flat out NO.

When I was employed as a bill collector it was drummed into our heads that if we EVER received correspondence from a cardholder that clearly stated we were not to contact them...we NEVER contacted them again, period, and end of story.

Credit grantors are so restricted with the legislation that exists to protect the debtor that they are ever so reserved, even restrained from using hardcore collections approaches.

Again...always send your correspondence certified, requesting a returned receipt.

Just because THEY won't contact you again after receiving your letter doesn't necessarily mean that they won't ship it off to a collection agency or attorney for *their* best efforts.

So if you think one little letter is going to get you off the hook, think again! The best mindset you can have is the one where the angel over your shoulder...the good conscience cherub, convinces you that you ran up the bills and eventually you will pay them back. Everything else will come so much easier once you've resigned yourself to that way of thinking. Your creditors are more inclined to do a little bending on your behalf provided they sense your intentions are admirable and sincere.

Q. If I don't think I owe a bill can collectors still "come after me?"

A. Here's where I'm going to ante up my two cents, ahead of the FTC. First off, there's no "thinking if you owe a bill" or not. You KNOW if you owe a bill or if there's been some mistake. There is a very good chance there may be a mistake, because the system is a series of numbers - account numbers, social security numbers, addresses, telephone numbers, you name it; and they all serve to create enormous margin for error during creditors' data processing.

More information on credit bureaus and various third-party reporting agencies can be found in Chapter 9.

You know this is all headed toward the letter righting route, but here's what the FTC says about it:

A collector may not contact you if, within 30 days after you are first contacted, you send the collection agency a letter stating you do not owe money. However, a collector can renew collection activities if you are sent proof of the debt, such as a copy of a bill for the amount owed.

Whenever "collection agency" is mentioned you may assume it is also referring to ANY collection agents, meaning debt collectors directly employed by the original credit grantor. This whole process is what is regarded in layman's terms as "filing a dispute!" As long as you are certain you do not owe a debt, regardless of whether your creditor sends you back their "proof" that you indeed owe it, stick to your guns. You are not limited as to the number of times you can reenter your dispute or lodge your complaint.

If your situation is "resolved" in the eyes of your creditor and they notify you within that thirty day period that they are reversing any credits placed on your account - that does not leave you dead in the water. The situation has to be resolved in the eyes of the disputing party, and that is YOU. It just means you are going to have to work harder to get them to see your side of the story.

Here's a perfect example of something that happened to me a few years ago in London, England while introducing that country to credit counseling as a consumer service:

I had rented office space downtown, in the financial district and purchased some paint from a local merchant. I have a penchant for trying to give my business to the "little guy" not only to boost local economy but because I know how hard it is to establish a Mom n' Pop operation.

Having gone through hundreds of color swatches I decided on a very pale and soft blue shade. I went down to pick up the paint in what is referred to as a Black Cab, loaded it up and headed back to our offices.

The elevator wasn't working (which should have served as an omen) so I had to lug the four *imperial gallons* up five flights of stairs. Imperial gallons are heavier than U. S. gallons, by the way.

Mind you, this story is without embellishment, although it might appear to be for the sake of driving home my point.

I opened can one and my jaw hit the floor. Inside this can was what could only be called *electric blue paint*. Back down the five flights of stairs, back into a Black Cab and back to the little merchant. When I reiterated that I was painting office walls and not a mural whose theme was the ocean floor for heaven's sake, it fell on deaf ears.

I was stuck with the paint because it was mixed especially for me. At least that's what the unnerving merchant said. He did have a good point, because NOBODY would paint ANYTHING that color.

Back in another Black Cab I hopped to one of those warehouse stores that have every item for home improvement under the sun.

Here's the bottom line: I filed a formal dispute, **sending it registered mail** to the owner of the company. Therein I explained my dilemma and even though we had a few words for one another in the store the day before, I was sure he owed me a credit for all the wrong paint.

His son admitted to me that Dad was a little hard of hearing and that it could have been his mistake ultimately, but Dad was the owner and it seemed the relationship he had with his own son was more tenuous than the one we were establishing right there.

And to think, from the beginning, I just wanted to do my part to help keep this local businessman's doors open. In summary: He responded to the chargeback and contacted my Visa Company who in turn **reversed the chargeback** they had issued to my account.

It took over a year to get that mess worked out in my favor, obviously extending the so-called "30-Day Rule" by a wide margin; and THAT is precisely my point.

If you know in your heart of hearts that you do not owe a bill, I don't care how long it takes you to get them to see the light; I am telling you **NOT TO PAY IT AT ALL!**

If you do lose your will to fight and make a payment for an item you do not owe, guess what? You are essentially telling your creditor that you owed it all along.

By making a solitary payment you have sealed your fate and until that balance is paid in full you can expect to be hounded and pounded for payment every single month. Do not make that fatal mistake.

Q. **Is there a late Carlin-esque list of words that collectors may not use?**

A. YES. It is identical to the late, great comedian George Carlin's list of words you can't say on television and it holds true today - even though some of the words on George's list are now acceptable on TV. Aside from those No-No's there are a number of other things they cannot get away with.

For example: A bill collector can't misrepresent him/herself in any way, shape or form. *They cannot say they work for a credit bureau if they do not* - and they don't because credit bureaus do not have the authority to make collection calls.

They cannot give you the impression that they are attorneys or working for an attorney's office if they are not.

They can't say you are being sued or threaten to take legal action against you.

They can't say they are going to come and put a padlock on your door and cart you off to prison for having an outstanding debt.

It sounds outrageous, but these styles are still popular to this day. And while most debtors are savvy and know they have "certain rights" that doesn't deter most bill collectors one iota.

The best and perhaps the most popular tactic of misrepresentation is the one where the collector says he/she is from a sweepstakes company and would like to talk to the head of the household - so they may inform them of their winnings.

If my wife or kid failed to hand me the phone for THAT I would have a fit. That is, I would have had I not been familiar with the ploy. And who wouldn't for that matter? That type of news is always nice to hear, but it tends to be a supreme let down when some bill collector on the other end speaks in a "gotcha!" tone of voice once you finally pick up the telephone.

If a bill collector calls you, whether they be from an attorney's office or not, they *may* inform you that you are about to be sued, but they may do so ONLY IF that is their intention. **May** is a key word to look for in their correspondence too, because it does not imply that they **will** do anything, which covers their behinds.

They cannot idly threaten to sue you in an attempt to "shake you up either!"

They are also prohibited from misrepresenting the amount you owe.

A collector cannot publish your debt in ways that are not compliant with the FDCPA.

Sure, they are entitled to report your debt to credit bureaus, but *they are barred from taking out ads in newspapers or dispensing information about you to any public forums*. No doubt this portion of the legislation was taken directly from instances where collectors actually DID perform those illegal tactics.

It also speaks directly to the laws pertaining to 3rd party disclosure.

Nobody is entitled to deposit a post-dated check prior to the date specified on the check.

Hold it right there!

There is never a proper time to issue a post dated check!

There is one reason and one reason alone for a collector to ask you to send a post-dated check:

That is - to have you over a barrel.

They know they cannot submit the check ahead of schedule, and that is a part of the law they never violate, however, most consumers don't know that *they* can stop payment on the check if the funds aren't available on the date it is scheduled to be put through.

I can think of NO CIRCUMSTANCES that would ever bring me to recommend the issuing of a post-dated check.

And since I haven't been able to come up with a single reason to do so up to now, it is doubtful that anyone can present a scenario under which it would make sense any more today than it did in the entire history of the world.

The psychology behind agreeing to issue a post-dated check, from the debtor's perspective, is understandable in the sense that at least you are able to temporarily get the collector off the phone and your back. You've given them an answer they can swallow and now you can go back to the table and have an easier time swallowing your dinner.

I have averred many times that you never want to give an answer just for the sake of avoiding confrontation. Once you've made a commitment you are going to be held to it and unless you've done a fair and deliberate assessment of your situation, you are not in the position to make *any* "deals" yet.

The psychology behind collectors requesting a post-dated check is to force you into a commitment, get you off the fence, prevent waffling on the subject and is a way for the collector to end his/her calls on what, for them, is a positive chord.

They are now able to earmark your account and don't have to deal with it until the date on your check. It lowers their bottom line for the time being because it comes off their list of accounts that need to be worked and therefore reflects a higher recovery rate for them. At the same time it serves to make them look better in the eyes of their boss.

Never knew it was such a competitive landscape, the collection biz, did you?

Unless you decide to stop payment on that check, they are already counting your money as theirs. There are a few matters about which I feel strongly and you might be able to surmise this post-dated check concept is one of them.

The following is a direct transcription of the Debt Collection Regulations as they appear in the FTC's Fair Debt Collection printout which is sent to consumers upon request: It is comprehensive and comprehensible.

The Fair Debt Collection Practices Act protects consumers from harassment and intimidation by bill collectors. It establishes a nationwide system for controlling agencies that collect other companies' overdue accounts.

Although many collection firms follow legitimate business practices, some have used unscrupulous methods in collecting debts. This law helps shield you from abusive treatment like threats of violence, harassing phone calls, all

forms of false or misleading representation, and the publication of "shame lists" of defaulting debtors.

The law is directed toward professional organizations whose principal business is collecting money from others. It does not apply to establishments that handle their own debt collections, such as stores, hospitals, banks and credit unions.

Under the provisions of the Fair Debt Collection Practices Act, after a collection agency first contacts you, it has five business days in which to send you a written notice detailing the amount of the debt and the name of the creditor.

You have the right to dispute the debt in writing within 30 days of receiving the notice. The collector then must verify the amount owed with the creditor and send that verification to you.

If you don't dispute the first written notice from the collection agency, the collector can assume that the debt is valid.

If you ask a debt collector in writing not to contact you, he or she cannot, except to tell you there will be no further contact or to inform you of plans to take specific legal action.

If you notify a debt collector that you dispute the debt, he or she can't contact you until they send you proof of the debt.

Another provision of the law is that a debt collector may not contact you at work if your employer objects. If the debt collector does contact an employer or friend, he or she cannot divulge that you owe a debt and can only use the contact to locate you.

Unless the debtor consents, or unless a court permits, a debt collector may not ask any employer to assist in collecting an employee's debt.

Further, the debt collector may not contact you at inconvenient or unusual times or places. For example, unless you agree, the collector may not call or come to your home before 8:00 a.m. or after 9:00 p.m.

The Federal Trade Commission is responsible for enforcing the Fair Debt Collection Practices Act.

You can sue a violating debt collector within one year of the date the law was violated. The debt collector is liable for your legal fees, and the court can award up to $1,000 in damages and additional damages for any resulting loss you incur, such as the loss of a job as a result of harassment.

Don't let the limitation of $1,000.00 stop you if your rights have been violated. I have seen cases where debtors have collected millions in punitive damages as a result of grievous violations of the FDCPA.

Q. Can my creditors report my debt to a credit bureau?
A. Sure. They all do. It is their way of keeping track of your payment habits and gives potential creditors statistics that weigh heavily in their decision to grant or deny you credit. For the most part, creditors determine your credit worthiness based on various criteria. Your rating of existing accounts weigh heaviest of all. Credit Bureaus are clearinghouses of information and, frankly, oftentimes misinformation. It would serve you well to pull a copy of your personal credit profile once a year. That way you won't be surprised by any information it may contain. There will be more on that issue in Chapter 9 as well. Being "reported" to the credit bureau can work FOR you…provided your credit is all up to date. But then you probably wouldn't be reading this book now.

Q. What is my recourse if I feel a collector has violated the FDCPA?
A. *You have the right to sue a collector in a state or federal court within one year from the date you believe the law was violated. If you win, you may recover money for the damages you suffered. Court costs and attorneys' fees also can be recovered. A*

group of people also may sue a debt collector and recover money for damages up to $500,000.00 or one percent of the collector's net worth, whichever is less.

Seems to me this question was answered about a minute ago; depending on the speed with which you read. Remember the part about being able to recover $1,000.00 a few questions back? And what exactly constitutes a group...more than one person? That means if I am a man against the world and I win my lawsuit I stand to glean a grand, but if I have a few buddies involved we cut up half a mill? You've got me on that one!

Q. What are some of the banned collection practices?
A. Several of the banned collection practices were touched on already in the answer to the question dealing with things a collector may and may not say over the phone. But here are a few more tidbits for you: They cannot make you accept collect calls or pay for telegrams they send to you. They cannot deposit a post-dated check prematurely.

They can't threaten to take away your home or property unless it can be done legally, and if that is the case, they must go through the entire legal process, inclusive of disclosures, notices, etc. A debt collector can NEVER say they are someone they are NOT.

Playing impostor was another tactic used quite a bit in the past, but since the FDCPA came about it has merely become a subject that old timers reminisce about around the water cooler.

All these items that are now considered torts are still tried out on occasion…on the occasion the bill collector thinks they have someone on the phone who's easy to intimidate or by his or her words display an ignorance about fair debt collecting that they feel can be easily exploited.

Debt collectors may not send you any package or letter that gives the appearance of being an "official" document if it is not in fact an official document.

A collector cannot send you mail contained inside an envelope that gives anyone the impression that the contents are from a collection agency or agent.

Example: If a collection agency's name is Genuine Debt Collection Services, the words Debt Collection may not be used on the outside of their envelopes.

They would only be allowed to use the words Genuine and Services, that's it! However, across the vast landscape there exist frequent double standards that leave me to somehow believe that if there was an agency out there called *Turnem, Ubside, Downe & Friskum* they'd be entitled to use their entire name.

Actually, that sounds more like a prominent law firm here in town. Whatever you do, though, don't confuse them with my pal's accounting firm: *Dewey, Cheatem & Howe!*

Q. Is it true if I tell someone I can't pay they can't bother me any more?
A. NO! Bill collectors do have rights too. Just because there is no debtor's prison in this country doesn't mean if you exhibit a super sassy lip they won't try to make your life a living purgatory.

It is always smartest to be courteous, calm and educated prior to talking to anyone about your bills. If you cannot pay your bills your last option is bankruptcy. You would better suit yourself by stating "I am sorry, but I'm not able to send the payment you're requesting. If you'd kindly give me some time to really mull over my finances, I'd appreciate it. Then, the next time you call me I'll be ready to offer you promises for payments that are realistic."

Typically, each account is pulled to "action" once a week, therefore, not only have you bought yourself some breathing room, you've established a decent rapport with the once-dreaded collector. Be as sweet as humanly possible.

Try a teaspoon of sugar first. If that doesn't work, blend in a tablespoon of honey or a few drops of corn syrup. And finally add a dash of sucrose. Notice my recipe's conspicuous absence of vinegar.

Your preparation, as a result of digesting the full course I've placed before you, should preclude you from ever having to sprinkle in even a pinch of bitters.

Your **Escape from the Plastic Prison** soufflé is underway.

Q. How can I report a collector who I feel has violated the Act?
A. Report any problems you have with a debt collector to your Attorney General's office AND the Federal Trade Commission. Many states have their own debt collection laws and your Attorney General's office can help you determine your rights.

Q. If I have any other questions about the FDCPA where can I go for answers?
A. If you have any questions about the Fair Debt Collections Practices Act, or your rights under the Act, write to:

Correspondence Branch
Federal Trade Commission
Washington, D.C. 20580

While the FTC generally cannot intervene in individual disputes, the information you provide may indicate a pattern of possible law violations requiring action by the Commission.

And here is their phone number: 202-326-2222.

I don't know about you, but if my rights are violated individually, I'm on the horn in a heartbeat, trying to get somebody at the FTC to work with me. It shouldn't matter if one or one million people encounter problems of a specified nature...selfishly speaking, if it happened TO me, I should receive proper attention from the authorities that can make things right FOR me!

Am I doing an about face here? Not really. I still want you to back up everything you say in writing. This number is an excellent resource nonetheless.

Chapter 8
CREDIT REPAIR CLINICS

Their industry name alone conjures up visions of faith healers who miraculously manage to perform open-heart surgery, using nothing but their bare hands and a little Baggie® filled with some red dye and a Play-Dough® organ of incredibly creative construction. Maybe these guys are *"plastic surgeons"* after all!

They promise to remove all of the ills that persist in your life that were caused by overextending your accounts, and they do accept credit cards as payment, ironically enough; although they'd prefer money orders.

From my experience, and from anything I've ever read about these companies, whether from credit bureaus, legal aid organizations, credit grantors or even their own advertisements and "unsolicited" testimonials, I can only classify them under the "If it sounds too good to be true, it probably is" category.

These CLINICS began popping up in the early 1980's when it became evident that the nation's consumers were spiraling out of control with discretionary spending at a rate that would make a carnival Tilt-A-Whirl ride appear comparatively tame.

A few savvy capitalists knew that eventually there would be a percentage (even if it was a tenth of one percent) of folks who just couldn't live up to their end of the repayment bargain.

The percentage didn't matter because one tenth of one percent of all debtors is still a monstrous figure, for their purposes.

They also calculated that there would be great numbers of people who, wracked with guilt, would not have the constitutional makeup to file personal bankruptcy.

They guessed, and guessed correctly, that most people would never learn that non-profit *credit counseling centers* were becoming more and more accessible to them. And by now you know how I feel about *that* industry's worth.

They surmised as much because most bona fide "non-profit" counseling centers could never afford to advertise their FREE or nominally priced services.

So those grasping at straws, those tiring of having to deal with the issue of indebtedness head-on, break down and avail themselves of these bastions of modern medical science, these miracle curing institutions, these all knowing, all caring **credit repair clinics**.

I ask these overnight phenomena the same question I got asked every day, "what do you do for people that they can't do for themselves," and their answer, if honest, has to be the same: Nothing, really! Only in their case, they revel in taking a great deal more financial pleasure in their work - because their charges are Mt. Everest steep.

It would help you to know exactly how they operate. Once you know, I think the chances are slim you'll be plopping your hard earned cash down on any of *their* desks real soon either. They are, however, thankfully, a vanishing breed.

Sadly, there are those that prey upon unsuspecting, uninformed individuals - and it always happens during the prey's days that are filled with trials and tribulations.

Can it be that people will spend upwards of $300.00 on someone or some company guaranteeing to remove bad information from their credit report forever? You better believe it! That's a mere drop in the bucket for someone who has been carrying the weight of the world around on his or her shoulders.

But what are they paying for and how does it work?

There are two basic ingredients in the formation of these companies. The key element is time, and the other is paperwork.

The FDCPA, while not the clearest piece of legislation on the books, is concise and strict in their approach to the proper reporting of bad debts to outside agencies.

You might recall that if one of your accounts is disputed, it cannot be reported negatively at the credit bureaus. Keeping that essential factor in mind; it is the very niche that the credit repair clinics have carved out for themselves. And *time*, initially, is on *their* side.

They have a three to six month window to do their dastardly deed, and, in most cases, fold their tent. The longest tenure of anyone I've ever seen in the biz is just under ten months. They've come and gone in mere weeks as well.

Read this little dialogue set in the Wild West, before the explanation:

"Help, I have fallen into debt and I can't get out!"

But you want to, even if it means not repaying your creditors; because you think this might be your easy way out. You heard 'bout one of them old fashion kind of elixir fellers once.

Enter the potion peddler hawking his wares: "Well, step right up young lady and young man; I have just the solution to pour down your throats! I will erase all of the bad credit from your reports for a handsome, but well worthwhile fee!" "It will be as if you never owed anybody nothin', never!"

So, what's his spiel, this credit repair mad scientist, you ask?

It is simply a variation on the dispute theme, a bit sleight of hand ala the shell trick. Every one of these "clinics" was set up under the same guise. They manipulate the fine line between properly disputing your debts and stalling for time.

They file written disputes for every one of your accounts hoping that your credit bureaus will remove the information from their files - because they aren't interested in or are too lazy to do the legwork required on their part to investigate your claims.

They just remove the negative data from your file and never contact your creditors.

How legit is that? It is sensible, in fact proper, to dispute an account when you know it is reported in error, but to dispute EVERY SINGLE ACCOUNT when you know full well those accounts are your responsibility - I ask you, at what point in their lives did the credit repair clinician, or the consumer for that matter, since they go along with the scheme, lose their scruples?

It probably occurred somewhere between missing a rent payment and getting fired from another job.

Feeding off the downtrodden at one point in all our lives strikes us as wrong, if not unthinkable, but we do a quick 180 when the potential for making vast sums of money creeps into the equation. It is intriguing how the rapidity with which some attitudes and appetites alter when cold, hard cash comes into view. No longer are those weaker-minded souls happy to just make ends meet.

Now they push away from the table, grunting, as they wonder which caviar goes best with their $9,000.00 bottle of Baron Phillip De Rothschild, vintage 1948. Values distort and it's easier to rationalize away the pain of others once the interest starts accruing in *their own* bank accounts.

There are several of those "businesspeople" that have realized THAT KIND of money. Needless to say, I won't be recommending them any time soon.

They'll send letters to all of your creditors, putting them on notice that your accounts are in dispute…and the waiting period begins. You've already surrendered a handsome chunk of change to get the wheels turning, usually about half of their overall fee, so you patiently, at first, play out the string.

And what happens if your creditors prove there is no dispute?

Well, then you are what they call SOL – Outta Luck being the last two letters' representations. If the credit repair company is still in business after all of your "disputed" accounts have been proven valid, you can whistle Dixie on the mayor's doorstep until the cows come home after learning how to play Beethoven's 5th Symphony on a kazoo and STILL be SOL.

They will stall you longer than they've ever had to stall ANY credit bureau, and by the time you feel you are close to getting some satisfaction...poof! They are gone! The thief of Baghdad would be in awe, and you'd be left angrier than the day you stepped out for a few minutes and missed the "Prize Patrol's" visit.

There you have it, in a nutshell.
The way credit repair clinics work.

Time and hours of serious investigative reporting have brought about a lot of changes that help prevent these guys from walking into our lives; which is primarily why these cats are now on the endangered species list, thankfully.

Call my opinions on this matter harsh, but when you see as many people as I have who've been 3rd degree burned by these characters...it has such a fingernails on the blackboard feel to me that it makes it impossible for me to care what happens to these or any other classic advantage takers.

I've always pulled for the underdog, and right now *you* have to be classified in that category.

There might be one or two credit repair companies out of the vast number in existence that are reputable, deliver on their promises and do a lot of good for people; although I have not had the pleasure of making their acquaintance.

Chapter 9

THIRD PARTY REPORTING AGENCIES

- So many accounts; so many mistakes.

- So many disgruntled consumers; not enough caring customer service assistants.

- So difficult attempting to correct the errors of others; limited avenues of communication.

- So frustrating and time consuming to put forth the effort; what do you do about it? Read on.

Third party reporting agencies, or credit bureaus as they are more commonly referred to, are classified under life's necessary evils. We can't live with them and we can't live without them.

The main reason they have received such a bad rap over the years is because bill collectors roll their names off their tongues as a consequence for your poor repayment habits.

The first thing you hear is: "We're going to report your account to the credit bureau!" What debtors don't realize is that before your account is even open it is reported to the credit bureaus.

We get the impression from collectors that only when things begin to sour are the records being kept. Untrue!

If credit bureaus had any smarts at all, they would start a public relations campaign to clean up their image. It would disturb me no end if the general perception of my company was negative.

To an untrained eye, a credit bureau report, or personal credit profile as they are known in the industry, can be as easy to understand as hieroglyphics inside the great pyramids of Egypt. And not nearly as colorful! I liken it to what happens to me when I take that long, arduous trek down the canned vegetables isle at the grocery store.

Saddled with the task of finding one specific name brand container of corn feels as though I'm staring at the same square foot of space for as long as it takes the moon to go from sliver to full and back again. But like anything else in life, once you understand it…it's not so bad!

How many times have you heard? "We'll have to pull a credit report on you first!" At least dozens, right?

Depending on your age - maybe 20 times.

Depending on the extent of your debt or the rate at which you've applied for credit…closer to 50 times.

Your credit history *does* follow you wherever you go. Contrary to what many believe, if you move from one state to another...THEY DON'T LOSE TRACK OF YOU! Yes, Big Brother has one eye on you all the time and as Joe Louis once said about German heavyweight boxer Max Schmelling: "You can run, but you can't hide!"

Instead of looking at credit bureaus as the ogre in your storybook of life, let's try to gain an understanding of what they are all about.

Although I have never been interviewed alongside a representative of a credit bureau (because *they* would never engage me in a debate or casual discussion of any kind) I can state, with a fair degree of confidence, their overall function today is as a clearinghouse of information. They are charged with logging chronological data about your lifelong dealings with credit grantors from coast to coast and beyond.

When they were established, some over half a century ago, they were intended to be a tool *for the debtor*. As time passed, however, the tool changed hands and their lifeblood courses through their veins as a result of fees received by *creditors* for membership; making it more of a fraternal organization than a public resource.

Is it any wonder then, why it's usually more difficult for you, the individual consumer, to receive adequate customer service and why a simple phone call by a creditor gets them practically whatever information they desire?

The activities of Third Party Reporting Agencies are monitored and governed by the Fair Credit Reporting Act (FCRA).

Like the FDCPA, the FCRA was enacted in the late 1970's. There have been some minor modifications, but from the debtor's point of view things are pretty much the same today as they were back then.

These bureaus must not report any item as negative when it is engaged in a dispute; **in written form on a sheet of paper separate from the actual billing statement.**

Never write on a statement and expect an answer from a human. It is shredded in the mailroom a nanosecond after your check has been snatched from its innards.

You can turn it inside out and upside down and backwards, but when you do the Hokey Pokey and you shake it all around...that's what it's all about!

Even more important to you as a consumer is the Fair Credit Billing Act.

This can get tedious, but there is enough you should know about the people who are reporting your credit tendencies to the credit bureaus that it makes sense to try to muddle your way through it.

The following is the word for word transcription of the *Introduction to the Fair Credit Billing Act*, taken directly from Volume 1, Chapter 5, 5.01 of the treatise published by Matthew Bender in 1982, titled **DEBTOR-CREDITOR LAW**:

Consumer credit billing practices are regulated by the Fair Credit Billing Act (Act)1 and by Regulation Z.2 The Act and Regulation Z contain provisions prescribing procedures for the correction of billing errors,3 as well as provisions regulating credit reports,4 the length of the billing period in a credit statement subject to a finance charge,5 the crediting of payments,6 and the refunding or crediting of excess payments.7 The Act also contains special provisions relating to credit cards.8 Note that the Act is closely related to the Truth-In-Lending Act (TILA),9 in that the TILA requires creditors to disclose to consumers the procedures for resolving billing errors.10 The Act and the corresponding provisions of Regulation Z apply only to open end credit transactions, unless a credit card is used to obtain closed end credit.11

If you thought *that* read like quicksand you wouldn't want to stay tuned for *their* "definitions." If you are ambitious you can easily obtain a copy of the Act online. What it does in a billion words or less is ensure your creditors make an effort to work with you, trying to resolve any disputes you might have with respect to their billing.

Following are the three major credit bureaus and how you can reach them:

1. Equifax
   P. O. Box 740241
   Atlanta, Georgia 30374-0241
   (800) 685 1111
   www.equifax.com

2. Experian
   P. O. Box 949
   Allen, Texas 75013
   (888) 397 3742 (Experian)
   www.experian.com

3. Trans Union
   760 West Sproul Road
   P. O. Box 390
   Springfield, Pennsylvania 19064-0390
   (800) 916 8800
   www.transunion.com

You can contact them individually to find out what your creditors are saying about you and how they are reporting your accounts, or you can pay a quick and painless visit to the website www.freecreditreport.com and get them all at once; but you can only do this one time before this site starts charging you.

The first report truly is FREE; I tested it, received all three agencies' reports and was never up sold or contacted again. It's a good deal.

Should you find yourself in an Act-intensive mood, besides the FCBA and FDCPA you might wish to pull up the following Acts for the sake of learning more about your various rights under the law.

They aren't exactly Tolstoy or Chaucer, but it is informative reading:

Equal Credit Opportunity Act
Fair Credit & Charge Card Disclosure Act
Truth in Lending Act
Home Ownership & Equity Protection Act
Fair Credit Reporting Act
Fair Credit Billing Act
Bankruptcy Abuse Prevention &
Consumer Protection Act

Speaking of Acts and as a matter of public record (so don't shoot the messenger) the following report is to let you know that credit bureaus do make "mistakes" occasionally; and sometimes the litigation brought against them attracts the attention of the Federal Government.

On January 13, 2000 the Federal Trade Commission released information online with a headline that read:

"Nation's Big Three Consumer Reporting Agencies agree to pay $2.5 Million to Settle FTC Charges of Violating the Fair Credit Reporting Act"

The courts determined that the above BIG 3 reporting agencies were ALL guilty of non-compliance with an amendment to the Fair Credit Reporting Act that was passed by Congress and made effective September 30, 1999.

It was becoming far too difficult for John or Jane Doe to gain access to real people whenever they attempted calling credit bureaus, whether it was to try to resolve billing errors, question other incorrect data they were keeping on file or to simply ask general questions.

The courts ruled that indeed, they were not accessible to the consumer and apparently figured this hefty 2.5 million dollars fine would begin to right the ship and reopen communications.

A decade later it's hard to tell if it did any good. Lawsuits brought against credit bureaus aren't necessarily down, but if you extrapolate that 2½ mill over a dozen years or so - today's fine would be closer to 30 million, and no three entities want to absorb that kind of financial punishment; so let us presume that it did do some good.

According to Jodie Bernstein, Director of the FTC's Bureau of Consumer Protection *"The reality is that consumers never got the access to the consumer reporting agencies that the law guarantees. These cases demonstrate in no uncertain terms that it's time for Equifax, Experian and Trans Union to pick up the phone and meet their obligations to consumers."*

The release went on to say:

"The complaints against Trans Union and Experian allege that since September 1997 over a million calls to their toll-free numbers received a busy signal or a message indicating that the consumer must call back because all representatives are busy. The complaint against Equifax contains a similar allegation involving hundreds of thousands of calls by consumers to its toll-free numbers."

Equifax agreed to pay (like they had a choice) $500,000.00 in the settlement and Experian and Trans Union had to cough up a cool million each (like they had a choice either).

All three agreed, albeit by court order, to fully comply with Section 609 c (1) (B) of the Fair Credit Reporting Act in the future.

I guess we could conduct a little test to see how well they are adhering to things by simply phoning each agency's toll-free number. Go ahead, it's your prerogative.

The point about your relationship with credit reporting agencies/bureaus is that you shouldn't be timid in attempting to approach them.

If you have a complaint or a question that's bugging you about how one of your creditors might have ranked your account or if you know for certain an error in identification is being maintained among their records, write down all the things you want to cover and pick up the phone and be heard.

If, after all your efforts to contact either of these agencies fails to net results that satisfy you, and if your frustration is only exacerbated by attempting to reach them - you may file a complaint with the FTC either by phone to their Consumer Response Center or in writing:

(877) FTC HELP (382 4357)
Consumer Response Center
Federal Trade Commission
600 Pennsylvania Avenue NW
Washington, D.C. 20580

The FTC also maintains a website and may be contacted online at www.ftc.org. All you have to do is point and click until you find their "Online Complaint Form." If you would like to purchase reasonably priced and worthwhile booklets from the FTC you may do so online as well.

The FTC is constantly in touch with your concerns and does a terrific job of addressing them in a comprehensive, easy to access format online. They see to it that credit bureaus ARE there for the consumer - as they were meant to be when first established.

Interpreting your credit report:

Naturally the first bits of information contained in your report are all about who you are. Your full name, address, date of birth, social security number and telephone numbers dating back to your great grandmother's first telephone that she had to hold in both hands and scream into to make a call...or so it seems.

CAUTION: If you have a common name, say John Smith, there is a strong chance that another John Smith's information may have attached itself to your file.

Even though no two individuals have the same social security number and something like mistaken identity shouldn't occur, it does. It does because they still have actual people manning the desks at the credit bureaus and we humans still make mistakes from time to time; being human and all.

If misinformation as simple as mistaken identity is reported, it "should be" rather easy for you to rectify in a single phone call to the credit bureau that maintains that specific account.

If the bureau is reporting **derogatory information** on your credit profile that truly belongs to the other John Smith you may have your work cut out for you to get it expunged. Start with the simple phone call and see where it leads from there.

Depending on the frequency with which you either apply for or are granted credit, and the reporting tendencies of the bureau handling your accounts, it is likely your place of employment's phone number will also be listed on your personal credit profile.

The next major element of your report is the actual data concerning your existing accounts.

Contained therein is specific information as to when you opened each account, the original line of credit extended to you, the date of highest outstanding balance and the all important payment history of every account you've had over the past seven years.

Seven years is the magic number length of time, by law, that negative or derogatory information can remain a part of your credit profile.

Positive information can stay on your report forever, and if you've recently slipped and now have negative items appearing on your file, it is good to be able to point out the fact that up until now you had always maintained an excellent repayment history; because the credit industry is based on the here and now or "what have you done lately" concept.

As far as the ratings and designations that are usually found to the right after all the individual creditor information are concerned, think 1 as being the best and 9 as the worst.

An R-1 (R standing for Revolving account) means you are making regular payments in accordance with the creditor agreement. At the bottom end of the spectrum, the 9 means that your account has been "Charged Off" and is considered a "bad debt." Between 1 and 9 it's merely a sliding scale from best to worst. Accounts whose numbers are preceded by the capital letter I means that they are Installment accounts, usually loans.

As a consumer you are entitled to an annual copy of your credit report. If you've been denied credit for any reason your report must be furnished to you free of charge. If your credit is excellent (you probably aren't reading this book right now) you can expect to pay a nominal fee for each report.

Chapter 10
THE COURTROOM ISN'T JUST FOR LAWYERS

The thought of having to make an appearance in court, for most people, is a notion that immediately tends to give one a sense of anxiety. Those of you who aren't public speakers or are called upon to verbalize with little frequency know exactly what I'm talking about.

You would rather face a firing squad, unmasked, than face a robed magistrate of the judicial system. On top of that, you are eyeball to eyeball with a well-trained, seasoned adversary who has managed to pass the bar exam and gets paid to debate in the sterile environment of a courtroom that is totally foreign to you.

While plotting your *Escape from the Plastic Prison* you may find yourself having to go to court, and you should be ready for that eventuality.

NO, the court isn't just for lawyers and bailiffs and judges and policemen and government officials! The court is there for "the people" to ensure our opportunity for fairness under the law.

If you are a debtor you most likely will not have legal representation at your side. After all, if you could afford an attorney, you could have afforded to start making payments to your creditors and might not be in court now.

Nevertheless, no matter how hard you try to negotiate a payment plan with your creditors, someone may still end up litigating against you.

Regardless of the fact that you've sent regular monthly payments toward your account, if you deviate from the letter of your initial credit card agreement your creditor has the right to file suit against you for breech of that agreement.

So, if you were sitting there thinking "As long as I pay *something* they can't sue me" you're wrong. They *can* sue you and they *will* sue you - and in the worst case scenario, even if you've displayed courtesy and professionalism, your case may fall through the cracks and you'll find yourself staring up at this ominous figure presiding atop a fortress wall, feeling like the ground you stand on is connected to a trap door that's ready to drop you into a black hole if you make one erroneous physical gesture or commit a solitary verbal blunder.

Not a pretty picture I've drawn, but I am only the sketch artist here, rendering from the images you've constructed in your mind's eye; out of fear of the unknown.

Sketch pad and pencil aside, let me share a couple of short stories with you:

We had a client I'll call John Doe. John owed lots of money. John sought our counseling advice and wound up enrolled in a rigid monthly debt repayment plan. John was sued by one of his creditors and began to sweat over those details. He wanted to dig a hole and never come out. But John was not an ostrich. John's panic buttons were flashing. See John relax. How so? John felt comfortable knowing he had Credit Counselors Corporation on *his* side. We, my Dad and I, managed to slow down John's metabolism by letting him know that we would be there if it ever got to the point where he had to go to court. It got to that point and we were true to our word.

Try as we might, we couldn't convince one of his creditors that John was a good guy, that he was making regular payments through a respected counseling agency (a rating of R-7 at the credit bureaus) and that he really didn't have any desire at all to go to court. They sued John anyway.

So, we all went to court. That was the first time in my life I ever saw and heard a man's heart beating through his sport jacket. I know some of you are reading and relating to this story already.

Continuing…

The court has what is called a docket, a listing of all the cases that will be heard before the judge on that day. Depending on your luck, there will be dozens of cases called before yours. But your luck hasn't been exactly terrific up to this point, so you can assume your name will be called first, even though some guy whose last name is Aardvark is on the same docket.

John's was the fourth case to be called that day. It wasn't as bad as if his was the first name on the list, but he *was* the first person who showed up in his own defense. In less than two minutes, they got to our Mr. *Doe*, a *deer* and petrified man that he was.

When he stood to address the judge, rather when we helped prop him to his feet, the judge made a statement that instantly chilled him out. "Sir," he said. Imagine *that* - a judge calling *him* sir! "I want you to know that by virtue of the fact that you are even here today in *my* courtroom, things are not going to be as horrible as you might think." It was like handing him an oxygen mask and a towel to dry off simultaneously. We knew John would be all right, especially when he began breathing again.

Still, there was the adversary across the aisle, staring him down as if he'd just run over his family pet of fifteen years. For some reason these attorneys take other peoples' debts personally.

But at this stage our Mr. Doe seemed ready to dance. With his reassuring words, the judge had seemingly placed an invisible force field around John. His demeanor and mannerisms morphed him into the poster child defendant.

He was confident, serious, focused and professionally attired as we strongly suggested. And if you consider that besides his two marriages, this was only the third time he'd ever worn a tie in his life; he must have been ready to attend the ball.

I don't want to Chase down the name of the bank that was suing John, but when asked, their attorney stood straight and true, stating: "Yes, your honor, I am the plaintiff's counsel!" He looked cool. We all admitted that. But those were the last cool words that ever came out of his mouth.

The judge asked if John was the defendant and he politely nodded. The judge told him nodding doesn't translate well or even show up on the transcripts that were being typed by the "lovely court reporter, Linda right there to my left." A little air seeped out of Doe's balloon, but he spoke up, and, after the first syllables cracked ever so slightly, he was speaking like a real person.

We stood up beside him and His Honor asked rather pointedly what we were doing there. "Are you Mr. Doe's legal representation?" he said with some harshness. "Uh... (My voice cracked) no sir, but we have information that will prove important to our client's case."

At this point the judge had a puzzled look on his face. If we weren't attorneys, how could John be our client? After an elongated explanation of who we were, the services we provide, and what in the world we were doing there, the judge agreed to let us enter whatever documentation we felt would assist our client.

He also, graciously, welcomed us and applauded our standing by John in his time of crisis. He was astounded to know that we were there gratis.

But that split second when he questioned our appearance in his courtroom actually had *me* ready to visit the restroom down the hall. After all, contempt of court IS an option, and I feared this judge might have thought we were not taking his proceedings seriously.

Our defense was elementary and we appealed to the judge's sense of…well, judgment. The obvious first question was: "Do you owe this money?" John looked straight in his eyes and replied: "Yes your honor, I do." To which the judge asked: "Then why are we here?" John gulped and yielded to yours truly.

I stood and said: "Your honor, we are here because we worked out an arrangement with _____ (insert Mr. Doe's creditor's name here) on Mr. Doe's behalf for payments of $145.00 per month; and he has lived up to his end of the bargain, making sixteen consecutive disbursements totaling $2320.00."

"Mr. Attorney (we'll call him that to allow him anonymity for his lack of integrity) *knows* we have an agreement, but for some reason he found it necessary to bring this matter to court. So, here we are!" "Is that correct, Mr. Lawyer?" the judge queried.

This is where Mr. Lawyer blew himself right out of the box. He lied. He actually said: "No, I don't know anything about any special deal that was made here. I was just sent to litigate the thing." The THING? He was turning into Jell-O ® right before our eyes; as he stammered and rocked from side to side. I had to stand up and voice my vehement objection, in my finest Benn Perry Mason impression.

"Your honor, I can't really say anything other than this man is lying through his teeth. I spoke with him two days ago and told him it was ridiculous for him to fly down to Florida to sue our client because Mr. Doe was making regular payments."

"I even said he should go after the people who were dodging him altogether, and asked him to leave my client alone. He remembers that…ask him, sir, please." "Okay, I will" said His Honor. "Is this true Mr. Lawyer?" "Um…I might have talked to someone, but, uh…it probably wasn't about this case."

Boy, the smell of cooked goose was a treat to our nostrils. I leaned over and told John: "Put a fork in this turkey, he's done!" "I beg your pardon?" chimed the judge. "I'm sorry; I was just asking my client something!" I guess my stage whisper was more audible than it should have been.

We were armed with every cashed check as well as the signed, accepted payment proposal, and when the judge asked if we had any supporting documentation we strutted up to the bench and explained that each check that was sent and cashed was there in chronological order. But the icing on the cake was the accepted proposal.

His Honor turned to the plaintiff attorney's table and said: "Are you going to sit there and tell me that you knew nothing about this arrangement. ARE YOU?" Mr. Lawyer's knees buckled, probably from the weight of his tongue falling over his chin. He had no answer. He had no chance at winning this case. All he had was the hope that he wasn't about to be thrown in the cooler for impersonating an officer of the court.

His Honor: "I have seen enough here." Then he became very stern, almost as if he was agitated, and continued: "You are here representing _____ (Creditor's name here) and Mr. Lawyer you have done a dreadful job. Not only were you unprepared, you tried to cover your incompetence by lying in MY COURTROOM! Consider yourself lucky that I am not holding you in contempt. I find for the defendant, Mr. Doe in this case and…tell me something, Mr. Lawyer" "Yes?" "What do you show the balance to be on this account?"

After several seconds passed without a response from Mr. Attorney I rose and offered the amount…in the interest of saving the judge some time and to save Mr. Attorney from the slammer...because the judge was THAT CLOSE to locking him up. "$7851.00 is the balance, Your Honor!"

"Here's what I'm going to do, and I want you to listen very carefully" he continued. "I am herewith declaring this balance null and void...that means Mr. Doe does not have to make an additional penny's worth of payments on this "thing."

"Do you understand my ruling, Mr. Lawyer?" he added. "Yes sir, I understand" he said nearly trembling. "And there's one other thing I want to say here. I want you to go back to _____ (Creditor's name here) and tell them that you just wasted my time, the defendant's time, and the peoples' time with this nonsense - and if you EVER come back into my courtroom you had best be prepared or I WILL find you in contempt and have you taken out in handcuffs. Do I make myself perfectly clear?"

Our opponent looked liked Leroy Brown, like a "jigsaw puzzle with a couple of pieces gone!" He did manage to eek out one final: "Yes sir, Your Honor."

We were now John Doe's new best friends. He offered to take us to lunch. We declined when he said he would have to use one of his credit cards to pick up the tab, though. We shared a laugh. Of course, as all the infomercials disclaim, "your results may vary!" And I would guess that what happened to John Doe in the courtroom that day was quite unique.

My Dad left with John - and I stuck around, seated in the back row of the courtroom to listen to the rest of the cases. I was hungry to gain more experience, besides, I had a real buzz going from the result that was just handed down to us.

There were 23 more names called. All were civil cases, similar to John's. Not a single defendant appeared, represented or otherwise. In every instance, the judge banged his gavel, declaring "default judgment ordered." This means that the debtor loses, the creditor wins, and, court costs and attorney's fees are added to the debtor's balance.

There are two morals to this story –

1. Don't be afraid to go to court. You are not being tried for a criminal offense. If you are prepared and you've attempted to do the right thing up until your "day in court" you likely will prevail. **In over 40 appearances in well over two decades, when allowed to speak on behalf of a client, I'm happy to report we've pitched a shutout.** There are some strict judges who will not hear from a third party if they are not legal representatives…but those same hardnosed magistrates will ALWAYS give YOU equal time, which leads me to the second moral of the story.

2. If you try to do the right thing, the courts will work with you.

If you come to court prepared and with admirable intentions, nothing bad can happen. If you don't show up at all, you'll lose!

The last story wasn't given a Hollywood treatment for your reading entertainment and pleasure. Everything happened just the way it came out on paper; as fantastic as it might have sounded. But this story is down to Earth and very much in line with what you can expect should you decide to go to court on your own.

The other story:

In 1989 we filmed a one hour video entitled "Getting Yourself Out Of Debt…A Matter of Dollar$ and $ense."

We didn't sell any of them because the people who convinced us to fund the project ended up skipping town or closing shop around the time when they were supposed to surrender the money we gave them for 2500 *finished* video cassettes.

Instead we got 2500 printed covers and NO TAPES! At that point we were out of project capital and it got shelved. Besides, that was such ancient technology; seemingly light years before DVD® and Blue Ray® hit the market.

By this time you could have ordered it for your Kindle® or other device. I might eventually be persuaded into lending my voice over talents and turning this into an audio book.

Back to the story:

In the video we wanted to show people how to get out of debt. We wanted to teach folks that if they were honest, sincere and dedicated, their lives could revert to the days when they didn't have to deal with the kind of stress that came with residing in Debtsville, USA.

We conducted person-on-the-street interviews and found a lawyer willing to go on camera to discuss the virtues of seeking counseling and the vice grip that too much extended credit can have on all of us if we aren't extremely careful. With this video project we were cutting our own noses to spite our own faces; because sharing the process of getting out of debt with the masses meant they would no longer need *our* credit counseling services either.

Hopefully you can understand that my intention with this book, while it may aggravate scores of credit counseling top execs, has always been the same; to help YOU, the debtor.

In that video we featured a LIVE studio audience that asked many excellent questions and in one segment we were lucky enough to be invited inside a courtroom to observe the goings on.

Much the same thing happened when we were filming as happened when we were by Mr. Doe's side.

There were only 18 cases; a light docket that day. Only one defendant appeared. The other 17 were issued default judgments as expected.

The man who did show up was not exactly dressed appropriately for the courtroom. In fact he looked as though he hadn't had a shower in several weeks. Candidly, he was completely disheveled; yet he was given his moment in the sun.

You could tell he was nervous at first, but this judge was as nice as the one who ruled in our client's favor in the recently concluded story.

In this gentleman's case, he had no record of payments with him, no cancelled checks and no recollection of any conversations he ever had with collectors wherein he made arrangements to pay them back - because he apparently hadn't been willing to deal with the matter for a very long time.

The judge asked him what he was prepared to do and he claimed he couldn't afford to pay more than $10.00 per month.

The judge implored him, from the top of his head, to briefly list his fixed monthly living expenses.

The debtor offered the amounts he had to come up with for rent and electricity and those two figures alone were sufficient for the court. So be it! The ten bucks a month was deemed acceptable by the judge and repayment at that rate was so ordered.

The plaintiff wasn't what you'd call thrilled, because the shot he took failed. He counted on the very same thing happening with his case that occurred with the other 17. He counted on a no-show, but his calculation was off.

You see what just showing up can do for you?

Don't be afraid to go to court even if you go it alone!

You are working from a position of strength that cannot be bought, not even by hiring an attorney. The judge is going to see you as a somewhat frightened, but concerned individual, braving your fears and facing your accuser; especially if you are humble and respectful in his or her eyes.

The odds of you winning the court over are excellent; far better than, say…the Cubs EVER winning another World Series.

Chapter 11
CREDIT CARD FRAUD

You need never become a victim of credit card fraud.

You've stuck with me thus far, so heed these words:

As a means of deflecting any bad publicity for their horrible policies, credit card companies would, for years, lament that fraudulent charge activity was so rampant that it was a significant reason for drastically hiking their interest rates.

Publicly they'd cry that something needed to be done in order to stem the rushing tide of credit card fraud activity.

Having heard their bemoaning ad nausea, both from the mouths of their bill collection agents as well as their upper brass, I decided to put my head around the situation and in fairly short order came up with what I thought were three foolproof methods for radically reducing credit card fraud.

It was the summer of 1982 when I scheduled a meeting with the Southeast Regional Director of Credit Operations at Citibank.

I brought my ideas to Citibank because they were by far the largest credit card issuer on the planet and I figured I might as well start at the top.

In a nutshell, here are the three proposals I made that I was certain would curtail fraud activity across the board, not just for Citibank, but for the entire industry:

1. Include the cardholder's date of birth in their account number. It doesn't have to be consecutively, so that would-be thieves might figure out the code, but intersperse the eight-digit number among the entire 16-digit account number.

2. Make their credit card a photo I.D. card. Keep all the merchant information on it, but have "visual proof" of the card's owner.

3. Instead of insisting that cardholders sign the back of their credit card, instruct them NOT to sign it at all.

I had supporting reasons for all three. The gentleman I spoke with was Lawrence Pugh, VP Card Services. He vetoed all three of my constructive ideas. For the first proposal he said it would be too difficult to assign the eight-digit date of birth among the remaining eight digits that make up the account number.

He claimed the second proposal would be an infringement on cardholders' rights by putting their photo on their credit card. We discussed the difference between that and other photo identification but he remained steadfast in advising me they had no intention of using the idea.

Finally, he shot down proposal number three.

Sadly, I left with a feeling that I'd wasted my time and money travelling to propose my fraud-cutting measures.

He thanked me for coming and for my concern - but wanted to fervently reiterate he had no plan of bringing any of my fraud-cutting measures to the light of a higher authority.

Interestingly enough, however, two months after my meeting with Mr. Pugh, Citibank went ON THE AIR with a commercial bragging about being the first credit card to have their customers' picture on it, saying "Such a simple idea, it's a wonder no one ever thought of it before."

So, they ultimately used the one major idea of mine that I'd hoped they would, and that's good – because beyond a shadow of doubt photo ID credit cards have done a lot to curtail industry fraud throughout the world; which was my original intent.

I'm not terribly troubled for not being given a smidgen of credit for the suggestion. What always unnerved me, though, was how I was summarily dismissed by Citibank and made to feel as if all three of my recommendations were valueless.

I tell that story because as fraud relates to you, a real problem exists.

Whenever credit card companies gripe about fraud being at an all time high, the consumer is affected - by higher interest rates and other ancillary charges that are imposed to supposedly offset the fraud activity. It certainly seems to me that they aren't really concerned about fraud all that much, particularly since they don't take most suggestions from industry professionals that they know ought to work.

And if you thought fraud was an issue back in the 1980's, you can only begin to guess what a problem it has blossomed into since online became the "future" of banking.

The key to not becoming a victim of fraud should center on the person committing the fraud and not the victim. The problem is, when the card companies lose their battle with the seasoned criminal they look to you, the victim, to get compensation.

That's just plain wrong!

I submit that it's more of a fraud on the part of the industry perpetrated and perpetuated against the credit card carrying public when they attempt to go after YOU for

charges they know you did not make – rather than focusing their efforts on the actual fraud committed by the dude or dudette who knocked you upside the coconut and took your wallet.

If you will do as I suggest, then I suggest your chances of becoming a victim of fraud are far less likely.

Put the initials C.I.D. on the back of all of your cards (my idea too, incidentally) instead of signing them. It is common knowledge these days that you, as the cardholder, are asking the store clerk to ask you for a secondary source of identification.

It cannot hurt you in the least. It may slow lines up a bit during the holiday season buying frenzy but it's still not worth signing your card over.

The logic, of course, is that if you do not sign the back of your credit card, the crook has no idea how to sign your name.

There is one thing that might help the thief, and that's your signed driving license.

Even if the perp gets your license or anything else with your signature on it and figures out how to sign your name reasonably well, you still have recourse by signing an affidavit of forgery for all of the accounts affected and **you are still only**

liable for up to $50.00 total per account on a proven forgery. That is the law!

Consider yourself Little Red Riding Hood and the Wolves (the credit card issuers) are out there ready to pounce on you. Much like the quick fix credit repair companies, there are companies that have slick marketing campaigns that want you to buy their credit card protection insurance. **DON'T BUY IT!**

The Wolves offer this kind of insurance policy and I feel it is a gigantic con job. Don't get suckered into it; even if their print ads are catchy and their TV commercials are in vibrant 3-D!

Another surefire way you can protect yourself against fraud, and while it sounds elementary I'll bet you haven't done it yet, is:

On a separate sheet of paper list all of your credit cards and other forms of identification. Include their account numbers, expiration dates, security codes on the back, your password if it is an ATM card or a card that provides withdrawal privileges, and any other details that are connected to each of them.

The aggravation of having to reapply, recover and recall all of that information on the heels of being violated via robbery is monumental. I heartily recommend you accomplish that small, but significant task sooner than later.

Chapter 12
THE "BAILOUT" WASN'T ENOUGH?

While the banking industry is virtually, if not literally, going to that *hot spot in a hand basket*, corporate bigwigs in their infinite wisdom and total disservice to consumers managed to finagle approximately **seven-hundred billion dollars** out of the government to save banking institutions and various Wall Street entities.

Let me put that number into clear perspective for you. You probably do not own a calculator that can display it. In fact, I don't know anyone who owns a calculator that can display that number. Here's what it looks like:

$700,000,000,000.00

That's a 12-digit number, 14 if you count the two zeroes after the decimal point.

You know how people ask "What would you do with the money if you won the lottery?" Well, wouldn't you say the bailout the banks were given was tantamount to *their* winning the lottery?

What would they or could they do with that kind of money?

For starters, they raised the interest rates on their credit cards a few points because they KNEW that legislation was afoot that would limit their fine print charges.

Most lottery winners claim they'd buy a new car for their kid, pay off their home, travel, and basically do anything they wanted to do with the money for the rest of their lives – after the family and very close friends were taken care of.

They wouldn't pat themselves on the back, say they won the lottery and before buying that new car or house saddle their kid with payments on their present vehicle before giving it to the child. But the banks think bank first, customers second – which is really *last* when there's only two parties involved.

As of January 14, 2011 the population of the United States was 311,890,828 according to the U. S. Census Bureau's U.S. and World Population Clock. By the time this paragraph is finished it will be greater by close to 100, so let me get quickly to my point.

75.8% of the country is comprised of adults or people over the age of 18.

18, that magical age where you're old enough to fight and die for the country but you can't celebrate a conquest of the enemy over a cold draught at the corner bar.

Out of all due respect, my calculation therefore takes 18 year-olds into sincere consideration.

THANK YOU, veterans, for all you do to protect the freedom that we hold so dear in America.

Continuing the calculation:

75.8% of 311,890,814 = Shoot, my calculator doesn't even go up to a hundred million. Now I have to figure this out in my head. Okay, 312 X 75.8% = 236,496, so let's round that down to come up with 236 million adults in this country as of January 14, 2011.

What I would have done with the bailout money is divide it evenly among our adult citizenry. Unless the calculator in my brain is incorrect, if you divide 700 BILLION (the bailout figure) by 236 Million (the number of adults in this country) each adult would receive approximately $2,900.00!

Think a three thousand dollar check in the hands of every adult citizen in America might help jump start the economy?

It's better than turning it over to the banks that in turn use the proceeds to figure out new ways around their credit card interest rates and other limitations recently imposed upon them by the present administration.

By the way, now the total population is 311,890,924. We grew by 110 in the past few minutes - and that number is *after* the number of deaths that occurred in that same timeframe were tallied!

So, we'd each have to take a few bucks less, but still I suggest none of us would have any problem with the new, reduced figure.

I'm sorry (but probably not as sorry as you are) that they didn't put me in charge of distributing that cash. I'd have called it the **BAILOUT AMERICANS PERSONALLY AND DIRECTLY ACT (BAPADA)** - and everyone would have loved me.

"VIVA BAPADA!"

Now, I guess you'll just have to settle for this book, rely on your lucky numbers hitting at the chance rate of 175,000,000 to 1 and consider you have a much greater opportunity of winning such jackpots; because those odds represent a much lower number than the BAILOUT figure!

Since this effort is being concentrated on the banks that extend credit, whether via credit cards or small loans, I'll direct this chapter at them and leave the excoriation of Lehman Brothers, Goldman Sachs, et al to *those* experts.

Comedian Bill Maher refers to my personal two favorite banks as "Skank of America, and Shitty Bank" and I have a fondness for those nicknames, don't you?

He also refers to the mega-monstrous insurer as the "Notorious AIG" but I promised myself not to talk too much about insurance, and I'm sticking to my guns now.

Here's the point I wish to make about the banks to which you are indebted:

While you must admit a fair degree of culpability regarding your existing mountain or mole hill of debt, some blame has to be placed on the institutions whose names and logos grace your once powerful pieces of plastic.

With interest rates going through the roof, with all of their nearly hidden charges that are too numerous to detail in this forum, no matter what the outcome of your personal situation - rest assured no one will ever have to throw a benefit on behalf of your creditors. Have I said that before?

It is interesting to note that a bank can be well known for being based in Atlanta, Georgia – yet be on record as a South Dakota corporation.

You might be surprised to "Discover" that a company you thought was headquartered in your own back yard is doing business out of Delaware, being called a Delaware Corporation to boot.

Wouldn't it make more sense for a company that has its physical offices with thousands of staffers actually working inside them in, say Atlanta for argument sake - to actually be a Georgia Corporation?

Of course it would, to answer that rhetorical question, but here's why they aren't: **Usury rates vary from state to state.** And how that relates to you is simple.

Usury can essentially be translated to mean breaking the law by exceeding fee limits established by the state in which a corporation resides. Following is the actual definition, copied and pasted directly from the USLEGAL.COM website:

> Usury is a civil or criminal violation involving charging more than the maximum interest rate allowed by law. The rate of interest legally allowed is governed by state statutes. If a court finds that the rate of interest on a loan is usurious, the interest due becomes void and only the principal of the loan needs to be repaid.
>
> To constitute usury there must be a knowing and consensual obligation of the borrower to return the principal as well as pay an amount greater than lawful interest. The lawful rate of interest will be governed by the country in which the contract was made. Usury is usually only

considered a crime if a person is a "loan-shark" (someone in the business of loaning money at usurious rates). Banks and other commercial lenders generally are not subject to anti-usury laws, but are governed by the marketplace and the competitive rates based upon the Federal Reserve's rates for bank loans.

State laws vary, and often contain exceptions for various types of transactions, so local laws should be consulted for applicable requirements.

I had it right on the nose, but let's break it down, shall we?

The third sentence of the second paragraph states ***"Usury is usually only considered a crime if a person is a "loan-shark" (someone in the business of loaning money at usurious rates). Banks and other commercial lenders generally are not subject to anti-usury laws, but are governed by the marketplace and the competitive rates based upon the Federal Reserve's rates for bank loans.***

Why it is ***"usually"*** considered a crime when Vito on the docks is charging his exorbitant rates but it isn't when Mr. Wanker of America does it is beyond me?

Why the double standard?

And, as a darkly comedic sidebar, how many people that are indebted to Vito have EVER seen their "case" get to court?

Vito's recovery rate is either 100% or the debt is expunged...by his client *becoming a sponge* at the bottom of the nearest, or three counties over, river!

Why then is it that banks are privileged enough to take their corporate logo and fly their flag in a state thousands of miles from their actual location?

Doesn't seem fair, does it?

I subscribe to the theory that many banks are as guilty of usurious practices as our friend Vito. After all, their goal, while vehemently denied, is to keep you on their books FOREVER! That's even longer than Vito. Well, in most cases - where his clients don't become BARNACLE Bills, instead of merely PAST DUE Bills.

The line between loan sharks and bankers is not only fine; It Is blurry.

The National Banks of Take Your Pick are Delaware companies because the interest rates allowed to be charged by banking institutions in Delaware are significantly higher on an annual basis than where the majority of that bank's branch offices exist.

It is a simple question of dollars and sense; if you owned a bank you'd subscribe to the same policy. If you knew you could charge 28% annual interest by having your operation based out of New York, South Dakota, Delaware or Texas when the rate in your state is a mere 16-18% - you'd race to a realtor in Poughkeepsie, Minot, Wilmington or Dallas and have them start house hunting for you immediately. It's capitalism at its finest; the American Way!

If interest rates were all banks relied on to turn their gluttonous profits, while it wouldn't be considered acceptable by any stretch, it would at least be bearable. But, believe it or not, there are VPs all over the country staying out late at night and poring (or pouring) over their fourth martini, trying to come up with other fees for you to pay.

And the ones that think of them get promoted. **I'm guessing the ones that fail to deliver are turned into bill collectors**. Sorry, I couldn't resist taking another shot at those folks – I gave them too many pages off the skillet.

A brilliant article by Brian O'Connor ran in The Detroit News on December 27, 2010, the title of which was:

2010 Piggy Bank Awards – Big porkers include ATM fees, credit cards.

He had me after the introductory paragraph which read: "Banks are *hogging* capital, lenders are *squealing* about being forced to play fair, mortgage firms are *wallowing* in fraud and credit card companies are STILL inventing new ways to steal your *bacon*" - because I'm a sucker for plays on words.

GREAT metaphors and they're all very effective.

Even after the banking bailout, the billions upon billions of dollars that went to these banks to right their sinking ships, the *pig* in them reemerged within months. They went *hog wild* in their efforts to raise rates; rates that differed from the ones that the government was supposedly "clamping down on."

O'Connor goes on to share figures, citing sources such as the Bankrate 2010 Checking Study that revealed ATM fees leaped a full 5% from 2009 to an all time high of $2.33 on average in 2010. And woe be unto you if you happen to need an ATM that isn't in your bank's chain and use one from another bank – those "inconvenience fees" as I call them climbed nearly 7% to an average of $1.41 per transaction. Overdraft fees also broke a record high at $30.47 on average - and the list goes on and on.

All this is to illustrate that while rules that limit banks are beginning to take root, as mentioned earlier, there will always be backrooms, bar rooms and alleys filled with calculating bankers; turning the tiles of their abaci to find new ways to make us pay the price of doing business with them - above and beyond what is morally and ethically right or fair.

To support my earlier claim about fraudulent conveyance, the fraud being perpetrated by the banks, is the establishment of "Payment-protection-insurance" programs.

This is a scam of the highest magnitude if ever one existed.

Supposedly you buy this insurance which promises to suspend your interest while you're sick along with alleviating you of your minimum payment requirements.

BIG STINKING DEAL!

Go back to my chapter on letter writing; compose the one that fits your situation best, and DON'T BUY INTO PAYMENT PROTECTION INSURANCE.

If your bank won't suspend interest while you're incapacitated, they should be the last thing on your mind on your road to, hopefully, physical or mental recovery.

According to the Wall Street Journal, those Frankenstein's Monster (Wall Street Journal didn't call them that; I did) payment protection policies cost between 80 and 90 cents for every $100.00 of debt.

Therefore, if you have a $5000.00 balance, the cost to "protect" that balance is $45.00…PER MONTH! That's $540.00 PER YEAR! What happens if you, heaven forbid, stay healthy?

In 10 years they will have charged you $5,400.00 to insure the original $5,000.00 balance.

And that's just from ONE CREDITOR! Imagine getting suckered into that kind of deal with ALL of your creditors!

And THAT, my friends, is a lesson in Banking 101.

Bottom Line: While you're working your way to debt freedom, don't waste an ounce of energy or a moment's thought on how you might be negatively impacting your bank or creditor.

The fact of the matter is - the only time your creditors think about you is when they are brainstorming to implement new methods of extracting more Benjamins from your wallet or purse.

Chapter 13
DON'T FALL FOR THE OFFERS TO REESTABLISH

Your road to debt freedom might be a long one. Don't let all the hard work you put into the process go to waste by your inability to resist the temptations that your former creditors might place before you once they learn you no longer have discretionary debt.

I've counseled people that have said they would NEVER get credit cards again after they went through the rigors of paying everybody off, however, when push really came to shove - the idea that they could simply hop back on the buy now pay later merry-go-round and rationalize it all by saying that they'd "done without" long enough was the straw that stirred them into finding themselves submerged in debt once more.

Not a large percentage had that happen, but when I heard that even one out of any number backslid that way it cut me to the quick. If a credit counseling company really had its client's best welfare at heart it would be an industry that never wanted repeat customers.

But, such is not the case with credit counseling firms, generally speaking today – which is yet another reason why I repeatedly and unequivocally state my present disdain for them.

Just for fun, I saved several solicitations after filing personal bankruptcy and I want to share a few with you now, if for no other reason than to prove my point about the credit industry wanting back in your wallet eventually, NO MATTER WHAT!

Make no mistake, you WILL get these too, it's all part of the plan to make you an indentured credit servant for life...and beyond!

I spent the better part of an hour pulling apart a file folder full of solicitations and randomly selected a baker's dozen that were **never even opened**. I got to the point where I filed them away for posterity; and posterity came today. Those I'm sharing with you begin in May of 2007 and continue through 2009.

At some point (perhaps they knew I was writing this book) they finally caught on to the idea that I wasn't taking any of them up on their offers and quit sending them to me altogether. My will, unfortunately for them, was stronger than theirs. I'm proud of that!

First I'll quote the outside of the envelope, then excerpt from the contents inside each one. I was amazed at how much information they could squeeze onto the front, as might you.

1. **Envelope:**

    Congratulations Mr. Perry, Introducing rewards you can actually use...DIRECT REWARDS Discover Card. 0% on Balance Transfers until May 2007! NO ANNUAL FEE. You're Pre-approved!* Credit Line Up To $10,000.00.

Content:

Dear Benn: (We must be close, personal friends if they're calling me by my first name) Now there's a credit card with rewards that actually benefit *your* lifestyle (like they have a clue as to MY lifestyle) and *your* budget. This NEW Platinum Card gives you rewards for the things you buy everywhere Discover ® Network Cards are accepted. You'll earn points that may be redeemed for cash rewards, gift certificates and gift cards from your favorite merchants just by using your card for *all your everyday purchases*. **NOTE the not so subliminal ALL YOUR EVERYDAY PURCHASES THERE?** Then, get a load of this one: **Count on Us to be Upfront with You.** We want you to know that we have the right to change, in accordance with the Cardmember Agreement and applicable law, your APRs, fees and other terms at any time, for any reason including, but not limited to, any change in your credit history, credit obligations, account performance, use of your credit lines with us or any creditor, or our financial return. Payments are applied to balances with lower APRs before balances with higher APRs.

Isn't that adorable, how they <u>want to be up front with us</u> and then go into a disclaimer that's longer than their offer? Basically what they're telling us is that if we sign the card agreement it really doesn't mean anything as far as WE are concerned – because they can change every element of its makeup at their whim, leaving us no recourse.

Think the recent change in the laws had anything to do with their sudden desire to keep us informed? Think the crackdown in wording of their card agreements by the Fed has anything to do with their approach? Think people are finally getting wise to their promotional techniques? If you answered YES to all three of these questions you're either a born cynic or you've learned a few things from yours truly. I prefer to think it's the latter. But wait…here comes the second offer:

2. **Envelope:**

Citi Professional Card sm with ThankYou SM Network. You've earned the title. Time to reap the rewards. You could see a plastic credit card looking thing in the window and on that it read $100 Gift Card** and NO-Fee Rewards, No Annual Fee, 0% APR on Balance Transfers* until 8/01/07(see letter for details). And this was ON THE OUTSIDE OF THE ENVELOPE. Think my mail carrier KNEW I was out of debt after having a gander at this envelope from Citibank? Here's a bit of a disclaimer of my own: Right after I opened a small business account for a website I designed propositions such as this one started piling up, and in each case they were soliciting a company with no known corporate officers, addressing them only as Dear Business Owner. There's that personal touch again!

Content:

Imagine. The Citi Professional sm Card comes with an online expense organizer so you'll NEVER have to spend time WEEDING THROUGH YOUR statements again. You can customize expense reports by jobs, clients or business trips and/or organize BUSINESS EXPENSES for billing, reimbursement of tax purposes – all before your statement arrives in the mail. So you never have to spend precious time tracking business expenses EVER AGAIN! To sweeten the offer they give you 3 Thank You Points per dollar spent at restaurants, gas stations, on car rentals and at certain office supply merchants.* And you get 1 Point for every $1 you spend on other purchases.* This is great, then you can get your ENTIRE BUSINESS in debt by handing out Citi cards to every single critical employee of your company. How cool!

I've decided to stop at 2 instead of 13. What I have to say now is more important to you than including any more of these ridiculous offers of credit. All the asterisks and all the complimentary talk about how wonderful you appear in their eyes is so insulting it needs to be pointed out – in order for you to move forward in a positive direction.

You can't believe any of the posturing that goes on during the courting process to have you reestablishing credit with anyone. The statements that they make, preposterous as they seem, all have the underlying theme of making you feel good about yourself and confident in your ability to handle payment of your account.

You're an adult, they appeal to your sense of need to feel grown up and responsible; so they convince you that you know how to manage your financial affairs now and, most importantly...THEY WANT YOUR MONEY!

And you well may have a handle on your personal finances by this time, but your best bet is to turn your back and run as fast away from them as you can – until YOU know you're ready.

A very cautionary tale: Every time you fill out a credit application, whether you want this to be the case or not, an inquiry is sent to the credit reporting agencies that deal with your accounts. *That's what I meant before when I said* **even before your account is open it's reported to the credit bureaus**. If you apply for one card and get turned down It wlll appear as an inquiry and show up as *credit denied*. The next time you apply, the creditor to whom you are then applying will have that information and might deny your application outright on the principle that XYZ Company turned you down; so there must be a good reason for it. What you are in essence doing then is cutting your chances of obtaining future credit by over-applying.

An old argument used to be that "you can't even get a rental car in this country without a credit card." To a large extent that is still true today, therefore I recommend that you do reestablish your credit, but do so with a card that you know you can PAY IN FULL every month.

That way you will not incur finance charges or other fees typically associated with credit cards.

You then are using your creditors instead of being used by them – which had been the case for longer than you'd care to remember.

Chapter 14
WHAT'S NEXT?

Your period of incarceration was wholly determined by your degree of debt and your rate of repayment. During the course of the three or four years it might have taken you to get to the enviable position of being debt free many things have occurred. You will have gone over peaks and through valleys and weathered a few storms (either during your negotiations or in the payback process) throughout this program of self-help.

Allow me to be the first to congratulate you on a job well done. You are a prize pupil.

By now you will have learned that life can truly be lived without having the use of credit cards and it's entirely possible that you might have sworn them off for life.

If that is not the way you feel now, if you are confident in your ability to live within your means and are considering applying for a credit card to get back in "the real world" I have sound advice for you to follow as well.

Don't be discouraged if by now you haven't received the solicitations to which I previously referred. They'll come; they'll come before you know it. Be thankful that you've not been tempted up until the time that you are ready; or you might have *signed on every dotted line* out of weakness.

If you've come through this ordeal relatively unscathed and without having to file personal bankruptcy, reestablishing credit should not be a ridiculously difficult task. Even if your situation warranted filing BK, there's still plenty of hope for you too; it just may take a bit more effort.

Before I provide the letters to write that should help get you welcomed back into the world of credit with semi-open arms, take heed:

Allow several months to pass after you've zeroed out all of your balances. Get comfortable with the concept of not having any credit card bills to worry about. It's such a good feeling that it will make you think twice about submitting new applications for credit.

If the yen to spend returns after close to a year and you feel it is necessary to have a credit card to exist in today's world, it's alright, but just touch your toes in the water; don't dive into the deep end or this time you might not pop back up.

Revolving credit doesn't have to be a revolving door spinning at 100mph. On YOUR terms, with your new-found knowledge, go about seeking the credit that is right for you.

Ridding yourself of credit cards can be as challenging as conquering any habit that requires a 12-Step program. Falling off this wagon could be equally hazardous to your health, so don't rush things.

Take stock of your fixed monthly living expenses, your discretionary costs (those fun things that allow you to escape the rigors of your daily life, such as weekends away, those **wanted** as opposed to **needed** trinkets for your house or spouse, etc.) and decide If you REALLY want to start up again with credit cards.

If you're ready to rock new credit, this is for you:

Remember, it took you longer to pay your bills than if you had made all of your monthly payments ON TIME and in the amounts initially required by your creditors, therefore, your creditors have been first-hand witnesses to your staying power, to your dedication to the repayment program you structured way back when.

You are not a "cold canvas new account" the term for someone who has never had a credit card before. YOU have a history, and the fact that you eventually paid all of your debts IN FULL should hold you in excellent stead when you contact your previous creditors, (if they haven't already contacted you) or new ones for that matter, asking them to extend you credit.

First I would highly recommend, if you don't already own one, a cash card attached to your checking account from your local bank. All banks have them, and it helps you monitor your spending with the same applied theory of - if you don't have the money in your account, you can't buy it! Like the old days. It's not really a credit card, although most of them do carry a VISA logo on them and they can be used like a credit card only without having to pay ANY interest. Or, to paraphrase Yogi Berra, "it works like cash, which is just as good as money!" It is the best possible scenario for someone out to reestablish themselves.

Next I would consider applying for a department store charge from a company whose card you previously carried or a gasoline charge card first.

Then, I would suggest you contact the very creditors to whom you've been remitting payments over these past months and years. Finally, I would go for a revolving charge account with a company you've never dealt with before.

Here's my rationale for those rankings:

You already have my rationale for a checking account cash card so I'll continue with the department store notion.

Department stores are in neighborhoods, places where you live and work and shop on a daily basis. They have the mindset that even though you might have fallen from their highest graces at one point a few years ago...they still want you to be one of their cash and check carrying customers. You probably had your best negotiating luck with them in the first place because it all comes back to their wanting you back on their books once you've paid them in full.

That happens to be forward thinking on their part. They might not have been thrilled that it took you "so long" to pay them back, but now that you have, they certainly don't want to lose you to a rival retailer. They still wanted your business when you were strapped. When you were in the throws of repayment to them they didn't want you running to their competition with what little discretionary cash you may have had in your pockets.

If Sears was one of your creditors they'd do whatever they could to keep you as a loyal customer and heaven forbid jump ship to JCPenney or Kohl's, and vice-versa.

Developing customer loyalty is another reason why most department stores hold accounts "in house" for a longer period of time while a cardholder is delinquent in payment. They are more reluctant to turn over accounts to collection agencies or attorneys because they don't want to ruffle your feathers to the point where you choose to never frequent their store again.

And THAT is another example of the credit game going full circle!

I cite gasoline cards next for practically the same reason. They are in the neighborhood, you need gas, and they want your money.

The major credit cards are last because in my humblest opinion they are likely to get you back in debt faster as a result of much higher credit limits, higher interest rates and lower scheduled monthly payments - and if there's one thing I want to avoid it's YOU having to re-read this book a year after you've gotten yourself out of debt!

The process for re-applying with a creditor you've already worked with before is simple. Merely fill out their application and wait for a response. They have your credit history on file unless it has fallen off as a result of the statute of limitations expiring on your accounts.

The statute of limitations on all credit accounts is six years and nine months from the date of last payment, which is critical. If you made only one payment in six years, but you made that payment IN THE SIXTH YEAR, the statute starts anew from the date of that one payment.

If the statute has run its course, you'll want to apply with your former creditor much in the same fashion as you would to establish an account with a new creditor; and that is covered in the next letter.

LETTER INCLUDED WITH NEW ACCOUNT APPLICATION

Dear _____,

I'm including this letter with my application so you'll understand that I am endeavoring to reestablish my credit.

As you are undoubtedly aware, my credit has been less than stellar over the past few years, however, I was able to structure and stick with a repayment plan until the day came, about a year ago, when all my accounts were marked PAID IN FULL.

Granted, it took me longer to pay back my creditors than everyone involved, particularly me, would have liked; but the fact is I completely fulfilled all of my obligations.

From _____ (month) of _____ (year) to _____ (month) of _____ (year), I repaid a total of $_____ to _____ (number) creditors. Their records should all reflect my payment history, and while they may not all be showing my account to be rated the highest, they should all be showing zero balances.

I have learned a genuine sense of fiscal responsibility over the period of time that I was making payments, and would never consider applying for any credit without being absolutely certain of my ability to make restitution in direct accordance with its specified terms and conditions.

Thank you for your consideration. I look forward to your response.

Sincerely,

_____

If Chapter 7 or Chapter 13 Bankruptcy was your "escape" route, the following letter to prospective creditors wouldn't hurt you a bit to send. It may not work very well with creditors that were included in your bankruptcy – then again, you never know. They too might be ready to rope you back in!

LETTER TO PROSPECTIVE CREDITORS

Dear _____,

      I am applying for credit with your company in an effort to reestablish my credit. On _____ my Chapter 7 or 13 Bankruptcy was adjudicated.

      It has been over ten years since I've had any discretionary debts and my financial situation has improved to the point where my disposable income has increased significantly. (They like that; it means they can get first dibs on your newly fattened up wallet!)

      I truly have a handle on my finances and am looking to your company in the hope that you'll grant me credit and allow me to make a fresh start. Rest assured I would not apply for any item on credit without being absolutely certain of my ability to stick to the terms and conditions set forth in its agreement.

      Thank you for your consideration. I look forward to hearing from you.

Sincerely,

_____

This letter should also accompany your application. Its tone is definitely along the repentant line, but unless this prospect has a very real sense that you've mended your spending ways, you'll be waiting an extraordinarily long stretch of time before even receiving your rejection letter; let alone finding a fresh credit card in your mailbox.

To fire off a letter like this takes a healthy degree of humility, but if it helps you achieve your goal of reestablishing your credit, it's probably worth it.

I will reiterate this important point: You do not have to sign on the dotted line of the very first credit application you get your hands on. In fact I discourage you to do so.

Do your homework and shop credit card interest rates. You'll be surprised to learn of the chasm between one credit card company's Annual Percentage Rate (APR) and that of others.

You are now an educated consumer and you can proceed as a wise shopper; waiting until you find the card with the best rate and conditions for you.

Here's an idea:

Play a game that hardly anyone ever plays. The next time you pick up a credit card application tear the back page off that provides their Terms & Conditions - keep that tear sheet, and throw away the rest of the application.

Then, go to your nearest store that sells magnifying glasses powerful enough to view the surface of the moon (because the Terms & Conditions are in very tiny print).

Take the torn application and your Hubble Telescope home and **read the entire statement of Terms & Conditions word for word.**

You might wish to start this process early in the morning on a day you're off work so that you can complete the task before your normal bedtime.

Follow this process with several applications. When you compare them to each other you will find vast differences in very important categories. You should be looking for the APR first and foremost, of course; because that is the best indicator as to how much interest you will be paying on that account **if you do not pay the statement IN FULL each month as I wholeheartedly and vehemently endorse**.

I think they should call it the MPR or Monthly Percentage Rate to keep us from having to divide the number by 12 every time, but if you've read what creditors have done with my ideas in previous chapters you'll understand why I figure on just keeping that one between you and me for now.

The key here is to shop that APR extensively. The difference of one percentage point per year can add up to hundreds of dollars in savings - or overpayment, depending on the card you select.

235

Look to see if one particular card has what they call "variable interest rates," which are tied to the "leading economic indicators" and can fluctuate depending upon those indices.

I've never opened an account with variable interest rates. My luck, all indicators would immediately point to the heavens and my rates would skyrocket the first month after I managed to get the card.

Maybe you'll have better luck, so I'll wish it to you if you attempt to land one of these accounts. Proceed with caution, because to me variable interest rates are akin to balloon mortgages that become due and burst at seemingly the worst possible times.

Be on the lookout for what's known as the "periodic rate" which basically means they charge interest based on a certain number of days per monthly billing cycle. Those days fluctuate and ALWAYS seem to fluctuate in the creditors favor – so one month might be based on a 28 days billing cycle and the very next will be based on a 26 days billing cycle; **which delivers interest to their accounts two days earlier and increases the rate to you.**

Imagine that!

Study the categories marked "Transaction Fees" and "Other Charges" and be mindful of them. Most applicants don't come close to conducting the review of the card's Terms & Conditions that you are now conducting. Ferret out all of the financial implications before affixing your John Hancock to any application, even if it takes the use of a high-powered microscope!

MOST IMPORTANTLY:

Whenever it is humanly possible...

PAY YOUR BALANCE IN FULL EVERY TIME YOU GET A BILLING STATEMENT and you will avoid ever getting into debt again.

Alright, I'm done! This book is about helping you get OUT of debt, not helping you get back INTO it.

Consider this chapter to have been an added bonus; a sort of reward for your fine efforts.

Congratulations for taking the longer but wiser journey to debt freedom!

Chapter 15
IN SUMMARY

If you skipped right to this page even before reading the introduction, raise your hand.

I probably would have done the same too, after all, isn't taking the fastest route the good old American Way? But the fastest isn't always the best route; as you will witness with this book.

You will not find the answers to your situation in this chapter. I'm not going into specific detail here; rather I'm making general statements about what you would have learned had you read up to this point.

If you truly are interested in getting yourself out of debt and out from behind the concealing bars of your personal plastic prison – do yourself a tremendous favor and spend the time it takes to actually read the pages that lead up to this chapter.

See you back here in a couple of hours.

Presuming you have taken the longer route and read your way up to this point, awesome! You're ready for the summary.

You will have learned that there is absolutely no need for seeking out and then paying a credit counseling company, great reputation or not, in order to get out of debt, period.

You will have learned (through my two personal stories) that the credit industry is as ruthless, underhanded, self-supporting and reckless as any other entity that you might encounter in corporate America on a daily basis.

You will have learned that writing letters to your creditors is the best possible means of communicating your intentions to repay, settle, ask for relief in the form of a moratorium or completely expunge your debt.

You will have learned that regardless of what happened to you personally, your debt situation is not unique and that it's time to stop blaming your spouse, your creditors or yourself over your situation.

You will have learned that regardless of your standing, social status, earning ability or potential - EVERYONE needs a budget; and **you will have learned** how to structure and follow your own budget that takes into account all of your fixed living expenses.

You will have determined whether or not you have the funds necessary to structure your own debt repayment program to your creditors or if your only real option is filing some form of personal bankruptcy.

You will have learned a little bit about Madison Avenue and their ability to get inside your head to make you want to run outside with pockets or a purse full of credit cards and yell CHARGE at the top of your lungs, and **you will have learned** how to prevent the hype and peer pressure from worming its way back into your life.

You will have learned about the laws that protect you from unscrupulous bill collection companies and their agents, and that credit repair agencies don't do anything you cannot do for yourself either.

A light about credit card fraud will have shined upon you and you will no longer fear the repercussions of, heaven forbid, becoming a victim of fraud.

You will have learned how easy it is to STAY OUT OF DEBT once you've reached that promise land, and that will be your personal pat on the back for a job well done.

You will even have learned how to reestablish your credit if that is something you'd wish to consider down the road.

Embrace the idea that now is the time to captain your financial ship and set sail - following the steady course that this book maps out for you in step-by-step fashion.

It is my fervent hope that you are completely successful in your efforts to initiate and fully implement these tools I've provided; that you recapture a large degree of fiscal self confidence upon completion of the occasionally challenging, yet ultimately rewarding process contained within these pages.

Soon after you finish reading this you're likely to hear an advertisement for a credit counseling agency, a debt settlement specialist or some other self-purported debt relief guru.

If you're a sports talk radio listener it will happen for you even sooner. The companies that advertise on these shows know that the male of our species is forever in search of the simplest and quickest solution; regardless of the problem.

While they'll appear to be concerned about helping you, I promise you they are more concerned about making money off of you. You'll hear that through their company it is much easier, that it cannot get simpler than one small and surprisingly easy to handle monthly payment. Make no mistake; what you are doing by tackling the problem yourself will be infinitely more rewarding on many levels.

Besides, with today's technology you don't even have to mail that single low payment to "them."

In a few short minutes, from the comfort of your own home, you can set up regular monthly payments electronically to carry you through the duration of your self-structured repayment plan; conceivably never mailing out another payment or having to write another check again. THAT is as easy as it gets, my friend, and you did it all by yourself!

A sign knitted by my dearly beloved and long since departed Mom that was prominently displayed over our receptionist's desk for nearly three decades, and a statement which you've already seen several variations of by now read:

> **"Nobody WANTS to be in Debt…but it CAN Happen to ANYBODY!"**

Do not despair over debt. Do not lose any more sleep worrying about how your creditors are going to get paid.

From personal experience I solemnly swear that once all your creditors are marked **PAID IN FULL** the overwhelming stress that indebtedness carried with it will be eliminated from your life and years will be added to it.

Besides the marriage to my soul mate and the birth of my son, there's no greater feeling on Earth than being debt free!

Your prison gate is now open.

You are free to go!

Made in the USA
Middletown, DE
09 March 2019